Gretchen Bitterlin
Dennis Johnson
Donna Price
Sylvia Ramirez
K. Lynn Savage, Series Editor

Ventures

STUDENT'S BOOK

BASIC

CAMBRIDGE
UNIVERSITY PRESS

CAMBRIDGE UNIVERSITY PRESS
Cambridge, New York, Melbourne, Madrid, Cape Town, Singapore,
São Paulo, Delhi, Dubai, Tokyo, Mexico City

Cambridge University Press
32 Avenue of the Americas, New York, NY 10013–2473, USA

www.cambridge.org
Information on this title: www.cambridge.org/9780521719827

© Cambridge University Press 2008

First published 2008
8th printing 2010

Printed in the United States of America

A catalog record for this publication is available from the British Library.

ISBN 978-0-521-71982-7 pack consisting of Student's Book and Audio CD
ISBN 978-0-521-71983-4 Workbook
ISBN 978-0-521-71987-2 Literacy Workbook
ISBN 978-0-521-71986-5 pack consisting of Teacher's Edition and Teacher's Toolkit Audio CD / CD-ROM
ISBN 978-0-521-71984-1 CDs (Audio)
ISBN 978-0-521-71985-8 Cassettes

Art direction, book design, photo research, and layout services: Adventure House, NYC
Audio production: Richard LePage & Associates

Authors' acknowledgments

The authors would like to acknowledge and thank focus group participants and reviewers for their insightful comments, as well as CUP editorial, marketing, and production staffs, whose thorough research and attention to detail have resulted in a quality product.

The publishers would also like to extend their particular thanks to the following reviewers and consultants for their valuable insights and suggestions:

Francesca Armendaris, North Orange County Community College District, Anaheim, California; **Alex A. Baez**, The Texas Professional Development Group, Austin, Texas; **Kit Bell**, LAUSD Division of Adult and Career Education, Los Angeles, California; **Rose Anne Cleary**, Catholic Migration Office, Diocese of Brooklyn, Brooklyn, New York; **Inga Cristi**, Pima Community College Adult Education, Tucson, Arizona; **Kay De Gennaro**, West Valley Occupational Center, Woodland Hills, California; **Patricia DeHesus**, Illinois Community College Board, Springfield, Illinois; **Magali Apareaida Morais Duignan**, Augusta State University, Augusta, Georgia; **Gayle Fagan**, Harris County Department of Education, Houston, Texas; **Lisa A. Fears**, Inglewood Community Adult School, Inglewood, California; **Jas Gill**, English Language Institute at the University of British Columbia, Vancouver, British Columbia, Canada; **Elisabeth Goodwin**, Pima Community College Adult Education, Tucson, Arizona; **Carolyn Grimaldi**, Center for Immigrant Education and Training, LaGuardia Community College, Long Island City, New York; **Masha Gromyko**, Pima Community College Adult Education, Tucson, Arizona; **Jennifer M. Herrin**, Albuquerque TVI Community College, Albuquerque, New Mexico; **Giang T. Hoang**, Evans Community Adult School, Los Angeles, California; **Karen Hribar**, LAUSD West Valley Occupational Center, Los Angeles, California; **Patricia Ishill**, Union County College, Union County, New Jersey; **Dr. Stephen G. Karel**, McKinley Community School for Adults, Honolulu, Hawaii; **Aaron Kelly**, North Orange County Community College District, Anaheim, California; **Dan Kiernan**, Metro Skills Center, LAUSD, Los Angeles, California; **Kirsten Kilcup**, Green River Community College, Auburn, Washington; **Tom Knutson**, New York Association for New Americans, Inc., New York, New York; **Liz Koenig-Golombek**, LAUSD, Los Angeles, California; **Anita Lemonis**, West Valley Occupational Center, Los Angeles, California; **Lia Lerner**, Burbank Adult School, Burbank, California; **Susan Lundquist**, Pima Community College Adult Education, Tucson, Arizona; **Dr. Amal Mahmoud**, Highline Community College, Des Moines, Washington; **Fatiha Makloufi**, Hostos Community College, Bronx, New York; **Judith Martin-Hall**, Indian River Community College, Fort Pierce, Florida; **Gwen Mayer**, Van Nuys Community Adult School, Los Angeles, California; **Vicki Moore**, El Monte-Rosemead Adult School, El Monte, California; **Jeanne Petrus-Rivera**, Cuyahoga Community College, Cleveland, Ohio; **Pearl W. Pigott**, Houston Community College, Houston, Texas; **Catherine Porter**, Adult Learning Resource Center, Des Plaines, Illinois; **Planaria Price**, Evans Community Adult School, Los Angeles, California; **James P. Regan**, NYC Board of Education, New York, New York; **Catherine M. Rifkin**, Florida Community College at Jacksonville, Jacksonville, Florida; **Amy Schneider**, Pacoima Skills Center, Los Angeles, California; **Bonnie Sherman**, Green River Community College, Auburn, Washington; **Julie Singer**, Garfield Community Adult School, Los Angeles, California; **Yilin Sun**, Seattle Central Community College, Seattle, Washington; **André Sutton**, Belmont Community Adult School, Los Angeles, California; **Deborah Thompson**, El Camino Real Community Adult School, Los Angeles, California; **Evelyn Trottier**, Basic Studies Division, Seattle Central Community College, Seattle, Washington; **Debra Un**, New York University, American Language Institute, New York, New York; **Jodie Morgan Vargas**, Orange County Public Schools, Orlando, Florida; **Christopher Wahl**, Hudson County Community College, Jersey City, New Jersey; **Ethel S. Watson**, Evans Community Adult School, Los Angeles, California; **Barbara Williams**; **Mimi Yang**, Belmont Community Adult School, Los Angeles, California; **Adèle Youmans**, Pima Community College Adult Education, Tucson, Arizona.

Scope and sequence

UNIT TITLE TOPIC	FUNCTIONS	LISTENING AND SPEAKING	VOCABULARY	GRAMMAR FOCUS
Welcome Unit **pages 2–5**	• Identifying classroom directions • Identifying the letters of the alphabet • Identifying numbers • Spelling names	• Saying classroom directions • Saying the alphabet • Saying numbers	• Classroom directions • The alphabet with capital and lowercase letters • Numbers	
Unit 1 **Personal information** **pages 6–17** **Topic:** **Describing people**	• Identifying names • Identifying area codes and phone numbers • Identifying countries of origin • Exchanging personal information	• Asking and answering questions about personal information	• Personal information • Countries • Months of the year	• Possessive adjectives (*your, his, her, my*)
Unit 2 **At school** **pages 18–29** **Topic:** **The classroom**	• Identifying classroom objects • Describing location • Finding out location	• Asking what someone needs • Asking about and giving the location of things	• Classroom furniture • Classroom objects • Days of the week	• Prepositions of location (*in, on*)
Review: Units 1 and 2 **pages 30–31**		• Understanding conversations		
Unit 3 **Friends and family** **pages 32–43** **Topic:** **Family**	• Identifying family relationships	• Asking and answering questions about family relationships	• Family relationships • Family members • People	• *Yes / No* questions with *have*
Unit 4 **Health** **pages 44–55** **Topic:** **Health problems**	• Describing health problems	• Asking and answering questions about health problems	• The doctor's office • Body parts • Health problems	• Singular and plural nouns
Review: Units 3 and 4 **pages 56–57**		• Understanding conversations		
Unit 5 **Around town** **pages 58–69** **Topic:** **Places and locations**	• Identifying buildings and places • Describing location	• Asking and answering questions about where someone is • Asking and answering questions about the location of buildings and places • Describing your neighborhood	• Buildings and places • Transportation	• Prepositions of location (*on, next to, across from, between*) • *Where* questions

READING	WRITING	LIFE SKILLS	PRONUNCIATION
• Reading classroom directions • Reading the alphabet • Reading numbers	• Writing the alphabet • Writing numbers	• Understanding classroom directions	• Pronouncing the alphabet • Pronouncing numbers
• Reading a paragraph about a new student	• Completing sentences giving personal information • Completing an ID card	• Reading an ID card	• Pronouncing key vocabulary • Pronouncing area codes and phone numbers
• Reading a memo about school supplies • Reading a memo about class information	• Completing sentences about class information	• Reading a class schedule	• Pronouncing key vocabulary
			• Pronouncing *a* as in *name* and *o* as in *phone*
• Reading a paragraph about a family	• Completing sentences about a family • Completing sentences about your family	• Reading a housing application	• Pronouncing key vocabulary
• Reading a paragraph about a visit to the doctor's office	• Completing a sign-in sheet at the doctor's office	• Reading a label on a medicine bottle	• Pronouncing key vocabulary
			• Pronouncing *e* as in *read*, *i* as in *five*, and *u* as in *June*
• Reading a notice about a library opening • Reading a description of someone's street	• Completing sentences describing your street	• Reading a map	• Pronouncing key vocabulary

UNIT TITLE TOPIC	FUNCTIONS	LISTENING AND SPEAKING	VOCABULARY	GRAMMAR FOCUS
Unit 6 **Time** pages 70–81 **Topic:** Daily activities and time	• Asking the time • Asking for and giving information about the days and times of events	• Asking and answering questions about the time • Asking and answering questions about events	• Clock time • Activities and events • Times of the day	• *Yes / No* questions with *be*
Review: Units 5 and 6 pages 82–83		• Understanding conversations		
Unit 7 **Shopping** pages 84–95 **Topic:** Clothes and prices	• Identifying clothing items • Reading prices • Identifying colors	• Asking and answering questions about prices • Identifying the colors of clothing	• Clothing • Prices • Colors	• *How much is? / How much are?*
Unit 8 **Work** pages 96–107 **Topic:** Jobs and skills	• Identifying jobs • Identifying job duties	• Asking and answering questions about jobs • Asking and answering questions about job duties	• Names of jobs • Job duties	• *Yes / No* questions with simple present • Short answers with *does* and *doesn't*
Review: Units 7 and 8 pages 108–109		• Understanding conversations		
Unit 9 **Daily living** pages 110–121 **Topic:** Home responsibilities	• Identifying family chores	• Asking and answering questions about family chores • Asking and answering questions about people's activities	• Chores • Rooms of a house	• *What* questions with the present continuous
Unit 10 **Leisure** pages 122–133 **Topic:** Free time	• Identifying leisure activities	• Asking and answering questions about leisure activities	• Leisure activities	• *like to* + verb • *What* questions with *like to* + verb
Review: Units 9 and 10 pages 134–135		• Understanding conversations		

READING	WRITING	LIFE SKILLS	PRONUNCIATION
• Reading a paragraph about a person's schedule • Reading someone's daily schedule	• Completing a schedule • Completing sentences about a schedule	• Reading an invitation	• Pronouncing key vocabulary • Pronouncing times
			• Pronouncing *a* as in *at* and *o* as in *on*
• Reading an e-mail about a shopping trip	• Completing a shopping list	• Reading a store receipt	• Pronouncing key vocabulary • Pronouncing prices
• Reading an article about the employee of the month • Reading a letter about people's jobs	• Completing sentences about people's jobs	• Reading help-wanted ads	• Pronouncing key vocabulary
			• Pronouncing *e* as in *red*, *i* as in *six*, and *u* as in *bus*
• Reading a letter to an advice column • Reading a chart of family chores	• Completing a chart about family chores • Completing sentences about family chores	• Reading a work order	• Pronouncing key vocabulary
• Reading an e-mail to a friend	• Completing sentences about leisure activities	• Reading a course description	• Pronouncing key vocabulary
			• Reviewing pronunciation of *a*, *e*, *i*, *o*, and *u* in key vocabulary

To the teacher

What is *Ventures*?

Ventures is a five-level, standards-based, integrated-skills series for adult students. The five levels, which are Basic through Level Four, are for low-beginning to high-intermediate students. The Basic Level also includes a literacy component.

The *Ventures* series is flexible enough to be used in open enrollment, managed enrollment, and traditional programs. Its multilevel features support teachers who work with multilevel classes.

What components does *Ventures* have?

Student's Book with Self-study Audio CD

Each **Student's Book** contains a Welcome Unit and ten topic-focused units, plus five review units, one after every two units. Each unit has six skill-focused lessons. Projects, self-assessments, and a reference section are included at the back of the Student's Book.

- **Lessons** are self-contained, allowing for completion within a one-hour class period.
- **Review lessons** recycle, reinforce, and consolidate the materials presented in the previous two units and include a pronunciation activity.
- **Projects** offer community-building opportunities for students to work together, using the Internet or completing a task.
- **Self-assessments** are an important part of students' learning and success. They give students an opportunity to evaluate and reflect on their learning as well as a tool to support learner persistence.
- The **Self-study Audio CD** is included at the back of the Student's Book. The material on the CD is indicated in the Student's Book by an icon SELF-STUDY AUDIO CD .

Teacher's Edition with Teacher's Toolkit Audio CD/CD-ROM

The interleaved **Teacher's Edition** walks instructors step-by-step through the stages of a lesson.

- Included are learner-persistence and community-building tasks as well as teaching tips, expansion activities, and ways to expand a lesson to two or three instructional hours. The Basic Teacher's

Edition also provides teaching tips to address the needs of literacy students in multilevel classroom situations.

- The Student's Book answer key is included on the interleaved pages in the Teacher's Edition.
- The Teacher's Toolkit Audio CD / CD-ROM contains additional reproducible material for teacher support. Included are picture dictionary cards and worksheets, tests with audio, real-life documents, and student self-assessments for portfolio assessment. Teacher's Toolkits 1–4 contain worksheets for cooperative learning activities that reinforce the Student's Book lessons. The Basic Toolkit provides letter-formation worksheets and alphabet and word cards.
- The unit, midterm, and final tests are found on both the Teacher's Toolkit Audio CD / CD-ROM and in the Teacher's Edition. The tests include listening, vocabulary, grammar, reading, and writing sections.

Audio Program

The *Ventures* series includes the ***Class Audio*** and the ***Student Self-study Audio*** SELF-STUDY AUDIO CD . The Class Audio contains all the listening materials in the Student's Book and is available on CD or audiocassette. The Student Self-study Audio CD contains the listening material in Lessons A and D of each unit in the Student's Book.

Workbook

The **Workbook** has two pages of activities for each lesson in the Student's Book.

- The exercises are designed so learners can complete them in class or independently. Students can check their own answers with the answer key in the back of the Workbook. Workbook exercises can be assigned in class, for homework, or as student support when a class is missed.
- Grammar charts at the back of the Workbook allow students to use the Workbook for self-study.
- If used in class, the Workbook can extend classroom instructional time by 30 minutes per lesson.

Add Ventures

Add Ventures, available for Levels 1–4, is a book of reproducible worksheets designed for use in multilevel classrooms. The worksheets give students 15–30 minutes additional practice with each lesson and can be used with homogeneous or heterogeneous groupings. These worksheets can also be used as targeted homework practice at the level of individual students, ensuring learner success.

There are three tiered worksheets for each lesson, all keyed to the same answers for ease of classroom management.

- **Tier 1 Worksheets** provide additional practice for those who are at a level slightly below the Student's Book or who require more controlled practice.
- **Tier 2 Worksheets** provide additional practice for those who are on the level of the Student's Book.
- **Tier 3 Worksheets** provide additional practice that gradually expands beyond the text.

Literacy Workbook

The **Literacy Workbook** develops reading and writing readiness skills by focusing on letter formation, the conventions of writing in English, and the connection between written and spoken language.

For each lesson in the Basic Student's Book, the Literacy Workbook has two pages of activities focusing on key words and sentences.

- The left-hand page is for students who are pre-, non-, or semiliterate in their own languages.
- The right-hand page is for students who are literate in their first languages, but unfamiliar with the Roman alphabet used in English.

When appropriate, students who complete the left-hand page with confidence can move to the right-hand page. Students who begin with the right-hand page, but require remediation, can move to the left.

Unit organization

Within each unit there are six lessons:

LESSON A Get ready The opening lesson focuses students on the topic of the unit. The initial exercise, *Talk about the picture*, involves one "big" picture that creates student interest in the topic and activates prior knowledge. It helps the teacher assess what students already know and serves as a prompt for presenting key unit vocabulary. Next is *Listening*, which is based on short conversations. The accompanying exercises give students the opportunity to relate vocabulary to meaning. The lesson concludes with an opportunity for students to practice language related to the theme in a communicative activity.

LESSONS B and C focus on grammar. The sections move from a *Grammar focus* that presents the grammar point in chart form; to *Practice* exercises that check comprehension of the grammar point and provide guided practice; and, finally, to *Communicate* exercises that guide learners as they generate original answers and conversations.

In the Basic Level, Lesson B focuses on additional theme-related vocabulary, moving from a *Vocabulary focus* that presents new vocabulary in context; to *Practice* exercises that check understanding and provide guided practice; and, finally, to a *Communicate* exercise that guides students as they use the new words in simple conversations.

LESSON D Reading develops reading skills and expands vocabulary. The lesson opens with a *Before you read* exercise that activates prior knowledge and prepares students for the *Read* exercise. The reading section of the lesson concludes with *After you read* exercises that check students' understanding of the reading. The Basic Level and Levels 1 and 2 feature a *Picture dictionary*, which presents additional vocabulary related to the unit topic and a simple conversation. In Levels 3 and 4, vocabulary-building exercises occur in *After you read*.

LESSON E Writing provides writing practice within the context of the unit topic. There are three kinds of exercises: prewriting, writing, and postwriting. *Before you write* exercises provide warm-up activities to activate the language students will need and provide a model for students to follow. The *Write* exercise provides guided writing practice. In *After you write*, students share their writing with a partner.

LESSON F Another view has three sections.

- **Life-skills reading** develops the scanning and skimming skills that are used with documents such as forms, charts, schedules, announcements, and ads. Multiple-choice questions that follow the document develop test-taking skills. This section concludes with a communicative exercise that focuses on some aspect of the document.
- **Fun with language** provides interactive activities that review or expand the topic, vocabulary, or grammar of the unit.
- **Wrap up** refers students to the self-assessment page in the back of the book, where they can check their knowledge and evaluate their progress.

The Author Team – Gretchen Bitterlin, Dennis Johnson, Donna Price, Sylvia Ramirez, K. Lynn Savage

Correlations

UNIT/PAGES	CASAS	EFF
Unit 1 **Personal information** pages 6–17	0.1.2, 0.1.4, 0.1.5, 0.2.1, 2.3.2, 4.8.1, 6.0.1, 7.4.1, 7.4.2, 7.4.3, 7.5.1	Most EFF standards are met, with particular focus on: • Conveying ideas in writing • Cooperating with others • Listening actively • Reading with understanding • Reflecting and evaluating • Speaking so others can understand • Taking responsibility for learning
Unit 2 **At school** pages 18–29	0.1.2, 0.1.5, 1.4.1, 2.3.2, 4.5.1, 4.8.1, 7.4.1, 7.4.2, 7.4.3, 7.5.1	Most EFF standards are met, with particular focus on: • Assessing what one knows already • Organizing and presenting information • Paying attention to the conventions of spoken English • Seeking feedback and revising accordingly • Working with pictures and numbers
Unit 3 **Friends and family** pages 32–43	0.1.2, 0.1.4, 0.1.5, 0.2.1, 4.8.1, 7.4.1, 7.4.2, 7.4.3, 7.5.1, 8.3.1	Most EFF standards are met, with particular focus on: • Conveying ideas in writing • Cooperating with others • Listening actively • Monitoring comprehension and adjusting reading strategies • Offering clear input on own interests and attitudes • Organizing and presenting information
Unit 4 **Health** pages 44–55	0.1.2, 0.1.4, 0.1.5, 0.2.1, 3.1.1, 3.1.3, 3.3.1, 3.3.2, 3.4.1, 4.8.1, 7.4.1, 7.4.2, 7.4.3, 7.5.1, 8.3.2	Most EFF standards are met, with particular focus on: • Anticipating and identifying problems • Attending to oral information • Interacting with others in ways that are friendly, courteous, and tactful • Solving problems and making decisions • Speaking so others can understand • Using strategies appropriate to goals
Unit 5 **Around town** pages 58–69	0.1.2, 0.1.4, 0.1.5, 0.2.1, 1.1.3, 2.2.1, 2.2.3, 2.2.5, 2.5.4, 4.8.1, 7.1.1, 7.4.1, 7.4.2, 7.4.3, 7.4.8, 7.5.1, 7.5.6	Most EFF standards are met, with particular focus on: • Seeking feedback and revising accordingly • Seeking input from others • Selecting appropriate reading strategies • Speaking so others can understand • Taking responsibility for learning

SCANS	BEST Plus Form A	BEST Form B
Most SCANS standards are met, with particular focus on: • Acquiring and evaluating information • Improving basic skills • Organizing and maintaining information • Participating as a member of a team • Practicing self-management • Working with cultural diversity	Overall test preparation is supported, with particular impact on the following items: Locator: W1–W2, W7	Overall test preparation is supported, with particular impact on the following areas: • Calendar • Numbers • Oral interview • Personal information • Reading passages • Writing notes
Most SCANS standards are met, with particular focus on: • Improving basic skills • Interpreting and communicating information • Organizing and maintaining information • Participating as a member of a team • Practicing self-management • Serving clients and customers	Overall test preparation is supported, with particular impact on the following items: Locator: W1 Level 2: 4.2 Level 3: 5.1	Overall test preparation is supported, with particular impact on the following areas: • Calendar • Oral interview • Personal information • Reading passages • Writing notes
Most SCANS standards are met, with particular focus on: • Acquiring and evaluating information • Improving basic skills • Interpreting and communicating information • Organizing and maintaining information • Participating as a member of a team • Practicing self-management	Overall test preparation is supported, with particular impact on the following items: Locator W7–W8	Overall test preparation is supported, with particular impact on the following areas: • Housing • Oral interview • Personal information • Reading passages • Writing notes
Most SCANS standards are met, with particular focus on: • Acquiring and evaluating information • Interpreting and communicating information • Organizing and maintaining information • Participating as a member of a team • Practicing self-management • Serving clients and customers	Overall test preparation is supported, with particular impact on the following items: Level 2: 5.1	Overall test preparation is supported, with particular impact on the following areas: • Food labels • Health and parts of the body • Oral interview • Personal information • Reading passages • Writing notes
Most SCANS standards are met, with particular focus on: • Acquiring and evaluating information • Improving basic skills • Interpreting and communicating information • Knowing how to learn • Organizing and maintaining information • Participating as a member of a team • Practicing self-management • Teaching others	Overall test preparation is supported, with particular impact on the following items: Locator: W2 Level 1: 3.1, 3.2 Level 2: 2.1, 5.2 Level 3: 2.1, 2.2, 5.1	Overall test preparation is supported, with particular impact on the following areas: • Directions • Oral interview • Personal information • Reading passages • Reading signs • Writing notes

UNIT/PAGES	CASAS	EFF
Unit 6 **Time** pages 70–81	0.1.2, 0.1.4, 0.1.5, 0.2.1, 2.3.1, 2.3.2, 4.5.3, 4.8.1, 6.0.1, 7.1.1, 7.1.4, 7.4.1, 7.4.2, 7.4.3, 7.5.1	Most EFF standards are met, with particular focus on: • Attending to oral information • Identifying own strengths and weaknesses as a learner • Interacting with others in ways that are friendly, courteous, and tactful • Monitoring comprehension and adjusting reading strategies • Organizing and presenting information
Unit 7 **Shopping** pages 84–95	0.1.2, 0.1.4, 0.1.5, 0.2.1, 1.1.6, 1.2.1, 1.2.2, 1.3.9, 1.6.3, 4.8.1, 6.0.1, 7.1.1, 7.4.1, 7.4.2, 7.4.3, 7.5.1, 8.1.4	Most EFF standards are met, with particular focus on: • Cooperating with others • Listening actively • Reading with understanding • Reflecting and evaluating • Speaking so others can understand • Taking responsibility for learning
Unit 8 **Work** pages 96–107	0.1.2, 0.1.4, 0.1.5, 0.2.1, 1.1.6, 2.3.2, 4.1.3, 4.1.6, 4.1.8, 4.8.1, 4.8.2, 6.0.1, 7.1.1, 7.1.4, 7.4.1, 7.4.2, 7.5.1	Most EFF standards are met, with particular focus on: • Attending to oral information • Listening actively • Monitoring comprehension and adjusting reading strategies • Reading with understanding • Reflecting and evaluating • Speaking so others can understand
Unit 9 **Daily living** pages 110–121	0.1.2, 0.1.5, 0.2.1, 0.2.4, 1.4.1, 1.7.4, 4.1.8, 4.7.3, 4.7.4, 4.8.1, 7.1.1, 7.4.1, 7.4.2, 7.4.3, 7.5.6, 8.1.4, 8.2.1, 8.2.2, 8.2.3, 8.2.4, 8.2.5	Most EFF standards are met, with particular focus on: • Identifying own strengths and weaknesses as a learner • Interacting with others in ways that are friendly, courteous, and tactful • Monitoring progress toward goals • Offering clear input on own interests and attitudes • Organizing and presenting information • Reading with understanding
Unit 10 **Leisure** pages 122–133	0.1.1, 0.1.2, 0.1.4, 0.1.5, 0.2.1, 0.2.4, 2.3.1, 2.3.2, 4.8.1, 7.1.1, 7.4.1, 7.4.2, 7.4.3, 7.5.1, 7.5.6	Most EFF standards are met, with particular focus on: • Conveying ideas in writing • Cooperating with others • Listening actively • Reading with understanding • Reflecting and evaluating • Speaking so others can understand • Taking responsibility for learning

SCANS	BEST Plus Form A	BEST Form B
Most SCANS standards are met, with particular focus on: • Acquiring and evaluating information • Allocating time • Improving basic skills • Organizing and maintaining information • Participating as a member of a team • Practicing self-management	Overall test preparation is supported, with particular impact on the following items: Level 1: 4.2 Level 3: 4.1	Overall test preparation is supported, with particular impact on the following areas: • Calendar • Oral interview • Personal information • Reading passages • Time/Numbers • Writing notes
Most SCANS standards are met, with particular focus on: • Improving basic skills • Knowing how to learn • Organizing and maintaining information • Participating as a member of a team • Practicing self-management • Teaching others	Overall test preparation is supported, with particular impact on the following items: Level 1: 1.2 Level 2: 3.1	Overall test preparation is supported, with particular impact on the following areas: • Money and shopping • Oral interview • Personal information • Reading notices • Reading passages • Writing notes
Most SCANS standards are met, with particular focus on: • Acquiring and evaluating information • Improving basic skills • Interpreting and communicating information • Knowing how to learn • Participating as a member of a team • Practicing self-management	Overall test preparation is supported, with particular impact on the following items: Locator: W5–W6 Level 1: 4.2 Level 3: 4.1	Overall test preparation is supported, with particular impact on the following areas: • Employment and training • Money • Numbers • Oral interview • Personal information • Reading passages • Reading signs, ads, and notices • Writing notes
Most SCANS standards are met, with particular focus on: • Acquiring and evaluating information • Improving basic skills • Interpreting and communicating information • Knowing how to learn • Organizing and maintaining information • Practicing self-management	Overall test preparation is supported, with particular impact on the following items: Locator: W6 Level 1: 2.1, 2.3 Level 2: 1.1, 1.2, 1.3	Overall test preparation is supported, with particular impact on the following areas: • Calendar • Housing • Oral interview • Personal information • Reading passages • Reading signs, ads, and notices • Writing notes
Most SCANS standards are met, with particular focus on: • Acquiring and evaluating information • Improving basic skills • Interpreting and communicating information • Knowing how to learn • Organizing and maintaining information • Participating as a member of a team • Practicing self-management • Practicing sociability	Overall test preparation is supported, with particular impact on the following items: Level 1: 4.1, 4.2, 4.3 Level 3: 4.1	Overall test preparation is supported, with particular impact on the following areas: • Calendar • Oral interview • Personal information • Reading passages • Reading signs, ads, and notices • Time/Numbers • Writing notes

Meet the Ventures author team

Gretchen Bitterlin has been an ESL instructor and ESL department instructional leader with the Continuing Education Program, San Diego Community College District. She now coordinates that agency's large noncredit ESL program. She was also an ESL Teacher Institute Trainer and Chair of the TESOL Task Force on Adult Education Program Standards. She is a co-author of *English for Adult Competency*.

Dennis Johnson has been an ESL instructor at City College of San Francisco, teaching all levels of ESL, since 1977. As ESL Site Coordinator, he has provided guidance to faculty in selecting textbooks. He is the author of *Get Up and Go* and co-author of *The Immigrant Experience*.

Donna Price is Associate Professor of ESL and Vocational ESL/Technology Resource Instructor for the Continuing Education Program, San Diego Community College District. She has taught all levels of ESL for 20 years and is a former recipient of the TESOL Newbury House Award for Excellence in Teaching. She is also the author of *Skills for Success*.

Sylvia Ramirez is a professor at Mira Costa College, where she coordinates the large noncredit ESL program. She has more than 30 years of experience in adult ESL, including multilevel ESL, vocational ESL, family literacy, and distance learning. She has represented the California State Department of Education in providing technical assistance to local ESL programs.

K. Lynn Savage, Series Editor, is a retired ESL teacher and Vocational ESL Resource teacher from City College of San Francisco, who trains teachers for adult education programs around the country. She chaired the committee that developed *ESL Model Standards for Adult Education Programs* (California, 1992) and is the author, co-author, and editor of many ESL materials including *Teacher Training through Video*, *Parenting for Academic Success: A Curriculum for Families Learning English*, *Crossroads Café*, *Building Life Skills*, *Picture Stories*, *May I Help You?*, and *English That Works*.

To the student

Welcome to *Ventures Basic*!

Enjoy your book in class.

Enjoy your book at home.

Your book has an audio CD in the back.
Look for the picture SELF-STUDY AUDIO CD in your book. Then
listen to the CD, and review and practice at home.

Good luck!

The Author Team
Gretchen Bitterlin
Dennis Johnson
Donna Price
Sylvia Ramirez
K. Lynn Savage

Welcome

1 Meet your classmates

Look at the picture. What do you see?

2 Classroom directions

A **Listen and point.** Look at the pictures.

1 Look.

2 Listen.

3 Point.

4 Repeat.

5 Talk.

6 Write.

7 Read.

8 Circle.

9 Match.

Listen again and repeat.

B **Talk with a partner.** Say a word. Your partner points to the picture.

Point.

3 The alphabet

SELF-STUDY AUDIO CD **A** **Listen and point.** Look at the alphabet.

Aa	**Bb**	**Cc**	**Dd**	**Ee**	**Ff**
Gg	**Hh**	**Ii**	**Jj**	**Kk**	**Ll**
Mm	**Nn**	**Oo**	**Pp**	**Qq**	**Rr**
Ss	**Tt**	**Uu**	**Vv**	**Ww**	**Xx**
Yy	**Zz**				

Listen again and repeat.

SELF-STUDY AUDIO CD **B** **Listen and write.**

1. <u>A</u> n i t a   2. ___ a n i e l   3. ___ a i

4. ___ r a n c o   5. ___ e e   6. ___ a k i m

C **Write your name.**

_____

Talk with 3 classmates. Say your name. Spell your name.

Hello. I'm Anita. That's A N I T A.

4 Numbers

SELF-STUDY AUDIO CD **A** 💿 **Listen and point.** Look at the numbers.

1 one	**2** two	**3** three	**4** four	**5** five
6 six	**7** seven	**8** eight	**9** nine	**10** ten
11 eleven	**12** twelve	**13** thirteen	**14** fourteen	**15** fifteen
16 sixteen	**17** seventeen	**18** eighteen	**19** nineteen	**20** twenty

Listen again and repeat.

SELF-STUDY AUDIO CD 💿 **B** 💿 **Listen and write the number.**

1. _6_   2. _____   3. _____   4. _____
5. _____   6. _____   7. _____   8. _____

Talk with a partner. Check your answers.

Lesson A *Get ready*

1 Talk about the picture

A Look at the picture. What do you see?

B  Listen and point: area code • country • first name
ID card • last name • phone number

CALENDAR

JAN	FEB	MAR	APR
MAY	JUN	JUL	AUG
SEP	OCT	NOV	DEC

Welcome!
Meet our new student

I ♥ MEXICO

Ernesto

Ernesto
Delgado
(212) 555-8307

DICTIONARY

2 Listening

 A 🔊 **Listen and repeat.**

1. area code   2. country   3. first name
4. ID card   5. last name   6. phone number

 B 🔊 **Listen and circle.**

Useful language
Say *oh* for *zero*.

4   0   3
four   *oh*   *three*

1 a. 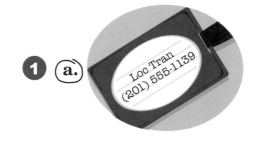   b.

2 a. 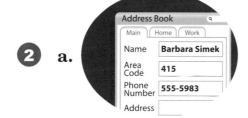   b.

3 a.    b.

4 a. 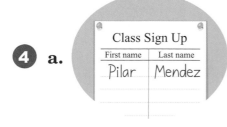   b.

Listen again. Check your answers.

C Talk with a partner. Point to a picture.
Your partner says the word.

Area code.

Lesson B Countries

1 Vocabulary focus

Listen and repeat.

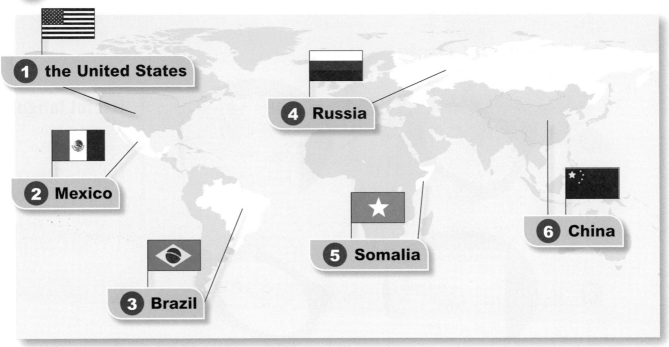

1 the United States

2 Mexico

3 Brazil

4 Russia

5 Somalia

6 China

2 Practice

A Read and match.

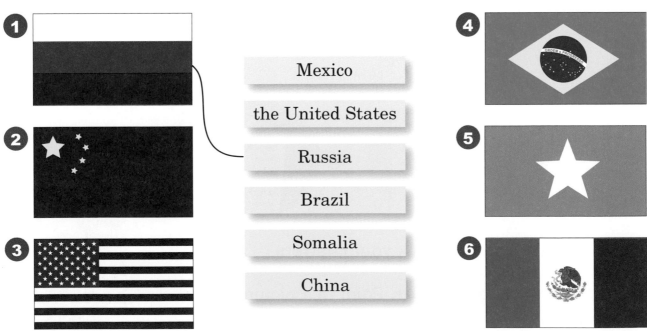

1

2

3

4

5

6

Mexico

the United States

Russia

Brazil

Somalia

China

B  Listen and repeat. Then write.

Name	Country		Name	Country
1. Ivan	*Russia*		4. Elsa	
2. Asad			5. Luisa	
3. Eduardo			6. Jun-Ming	

Talk with a partner. Ask and answer.

> **A** Where is **Ivan** from?
> **B Russia.**

3 Communicate

Talk in a group. Ask and answer. Complete the chart.

> **A** What's your name?
> **B Chi.**
> **A** Where are you from?
> **B Vietnam.**

Name	Country
Chi	*Vietnam*

What's your name?

1 Grammar focus: *your, his, her, my*

What's	your his her	name?

My His Her	name is	Angela. Kevin. Julia.

What's = What is

2 Practice

A Read and circle. Then write.

1

A What's your name?

B _____My_____ name is Nancy.
     (My) Your

2

A What's his name?

B _____ name is Chin.
     His   Her

3

A What's her name?

B _____ name is Alima.
     His   Her

4

A What's your name?

B _____ name is Vincent.
     My   Your

Listen and repeat. Then practice with a partner.

B 🎧 **Listen and repeat.** Then write.

Tops Adult School	
First name: Jack	
Last name: Lee	
Area code: 203	
Phone number: 555-9687	

Tops Adult School	
First name: Sara	
Last name: Garza	
Area code: 415	
Phone number: 555-3702	

What's his . . . ?

1. first ___*name*___	Jack
2. last _____	Lee
3. area _____	203
4. phone _____	555-9687

What's her . . . ?

5. _____ code	415
6. _____ number	555-3702
7. _____ name	Garza
8. _____ name	Sara

Talk with a partner. Ask and answer.

A What's **his first name**?
B **Jack.**

3 Communicate

Talk with your classmates. Complete the chart.

A What's your **first name**?
B My **first name** is **Yuri**.

Useful language
How do you spell **Yuri**?
Y U R I.

First name	Last name	Area code	Phone number
Yuri			

1 Before you read

Talk about the picture.
What do you see?

METRO ADULT SCHOOL

2 Read

 Listen and read.

SELF-STUDY
AUDIO CD

Welcome!

Meet our new student.

His first name is Ernesto.

His last name is Delgado.

He is from Mexico.

Welcome, Ernesto Delgado!

3 After you read

Read the sentences. Circle *Yes* or *No*.

1. His name is Ernesto Mexico.   Yes (No)
2. His first name is Ernesto.   Yes No
3. His last name is Delgado.   Yes No
4. He is from Ecuador.   Yes No

Picture dictionary · Months of the year

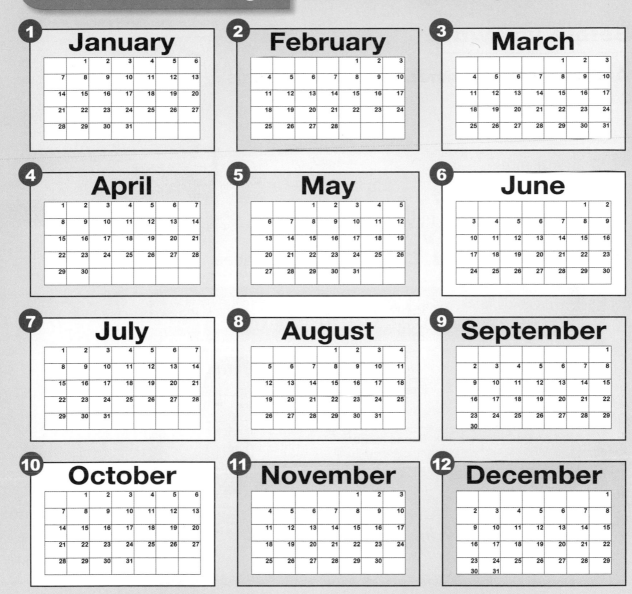

1 January

		1	2	3	4	5	6
7	8	9	10	11	12	13	
14	15	16	17	18	19	20	
21	22	23	24	25	26	27	
28	29	30	31				

2 February

				1	2	3
4	5	6	7	8	9	10
11	12	13	14	15	16	17
18	19	20	21	22	23	24
25	26	27	28			

3 March

				1	2	3
4	5	6	7	8	9	10
11	12	13	14	15	16	17
18	19	20	21	22	23	24
25	26	27	28	29	30	31

4 April

1	2	3	4	5	6	7
8	9	10	11	12	13	14
15	16	17	18	19	20	21
22	23	24	25	26	27	28
29	30					

5 May

		1	2	3	4	5
6	7	8	9	10	11	12
13	14	15	16	17	18	19
20	21	22	23	24	25	26
27	28	29	30	31		

6 June

					1	2
3	4	5	6	7	8	9
10	11	12	13	14	15	16
17	18	19	20	21	22	23
24	25	26	27	28	29	30

7 July

1	2	3	4	5	6	7
8	9	10	11	12	13	14
15	16	17	18	19	20	21
22	23	24	25	26	27	28
29	30	31				

8 August

		1	2	3	4	
5	6	7	8	9	10	11
12	13	14	15	16	17	18
19	20	21	22	23	24	25
26	27	28	29	30	31	

9 September

						1
2	3	4	5	6	7	8
9	10	11	12	13	14	15
16	17	18	19	20	21	22
23	24	25	26	27	28	29
30						

10 October

		1	2	3	4	5	6
7	8	9	10	11	12	13	
14	15	16	17	18	19	20	
21	22	23	24	25	26	27	
28	29	30	31				

11 November

				1	2	3
4	5	6	7	8	9	10
11	12	13	14	15	16	17
18	19	20	21	22	23	24
25	26	27	28	29	30	

12 December

						1
2	3	4	5	6	7	8
9	10	11	12	13	14	15
16	17	18	19	20	21	22
23	24	25	26	27	28	29
30	31					

SELF-STUDY
AUDIO CD

A 🔘 **Listen and repeat.** Look at the picture dictionary.

B Talk with your classmates. Complete the chart.

A What's your name?
B **Eva.**
A When's your birthday?
B In **April.**

Name	Month
Eva	*April*

1 Before you write

A Talk with a partner. Complete the words.

1. __*f*__ i r s t
2. ___ a s t
3. ___ a m e
4. a r e a ___ o d e
5. p h o n e ___ u m b e r

B Read the ID card. Complete the sentences.

Central Adult School Library

Wong	**Linda**
Last name	First name
916	**555-7834**
Area code	Phone number
China	
Country	

Linda Wong

Signature

Culture note
Your signature is how you write your name.

1. Her _____ _____ is Linda.
2. Her _____ _____ is Wong.
3. Her _____ _____ is 916.
4. Her _____ _____ is 555-7834.
5. She is from _____ .

2 Write

A Complete the ID card. Write about yourself.

Central Adult School Library

Last name _____

First name _____

Area code _____

Phone number _____

Country _____

Signature _____

B Complete the sentences. Write about yourself.

1. My first name is _____.

2. My last name is _____.

3. My area code is _____.

4. My phone number is _____.

5. My birthday is in _____.

3 After you write

Talk with a partner. Share your writing.

1 Life-skills reading

Midtown Adult School

NAME: Samir Ahmed

ADDRESS: 1432 Woodrow Street
Tampa, FL 33612

PHONE: (813) 555-6978

BIRTHDAY: February 8, 1985

Samir Ahmed
SIGNATURE

A **Read the sentences.** Look at the ID card.
Circle the answers.

1. His first name is ____ .
   a. Ahmed
   b. Samir

2. His area code is ____ .
   a. 813
   b. 33612

3. His birthday is in ____ .
   a. January
   b. February

4. His last name is ____ .
   a. Ahmed
   b. Woodrow

B **Talk with a partner.**

Say two things about Samir.

2 Fun with language

A What word is different? Circle the word.

1. Countries	2. Months	3. Phone numbers
Mexico	April	555-4861
China	September	555-6978
(November)	May	415
Somalia	Russia	555-7934

4. Area codes	5. First names	6. Last names
555-6948	Linda	Cruz
813	Alima	February
212	Nasser	Delgado
915	Mexico	Lee

Talk with a partner. Check your answers.

B Work with a partner. Write the months in order.

April	August	December	February	January	July
June	March	May	November	October	September

1 January	**2**	**3**	**4**
5	**6**	**7**	**8**
9	**10**	**11**	**12**

3 Wrap up

Complete the **Self-assessment** on page 141.

Get ready

1 Talk about the picture

A Look at the picture. What do you see?

B 🔘 Listen and point: a book • a chair • a computer
a desk • a notebook • a pencil

Ventures Basic, Unit 2
Pages 18 and 19

Sue

2 Listening

A **Listen and repeat.**

1. a book   2. a chair   3. a computer
4. a desk   5. a notebook   6. a pencil

B **Listen and circle.**

1 a.    (b.)

2 a.    b.

3 a.    b.

4 a.    b.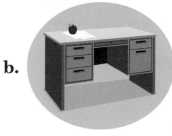

A desk.

Listen again. Check your answers.

C **Talk with a partner.** Point to a picture.
Your partner says the word.

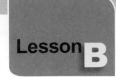

Classroom objects

1 Vocabulary focus

💿 **Listen and repeat.**

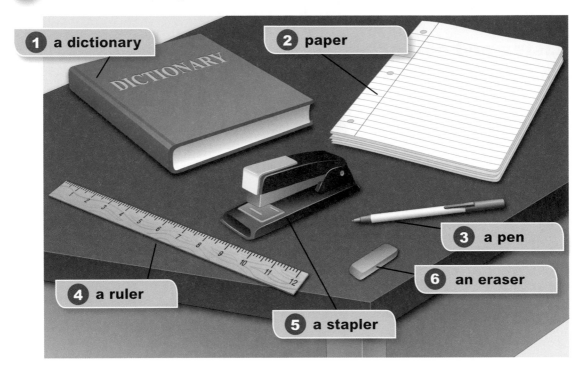

1 a dictionary

2 paper

3 a pen

4 a ruler

5 a stapler

6 an eraser

2 Practice

A Read and match.

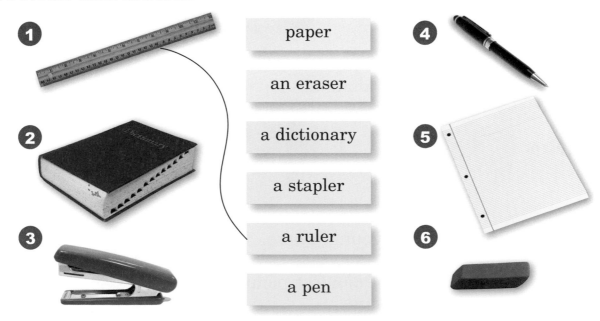

1

2

3

paper

an eraser

a dictionary

a stapler

a ruler

a pen

4

5

6

B 🔊 **Listen and repeat.** Then write.

a dictionary	an eraser	paper
a pen	a ruler	a stapler

1. *a dictionary*
2.
3.
4.
5.
6.

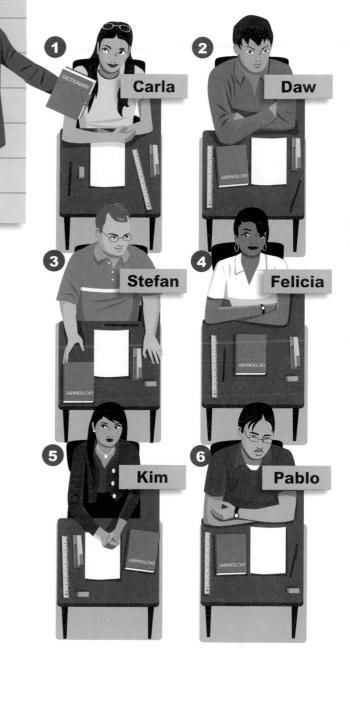

① Carla

② Daw

③ Stefan

④ Felicia

⑤ Kim

⑥ Pablo

Talk with a partner.
Act it out.

A What do you need, **Carla**?
B **A dictionary.**
A Here you are.

3 Communicate

Talk with your classmates.
Complete the chart.

A What do you need, **Mahmoud**?
B **An eraser.**

Name	Classroom object
Mahmoud	an eraser

Where's my pencil?

1 Grammar focus: *in* and *on*

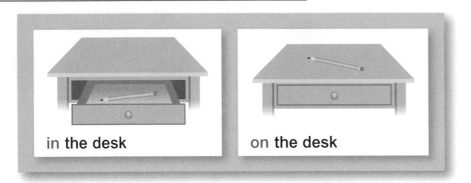

in the desk   on the desk

2 Practice

A Read and circle. Then write.

1. **A** Where's my pencil?
   B ____*In*____ the desk.
      (In) On

2. **A** Where's my notebook?
   B _____ the desk.
      In   On

3. **A** Where's my pen?
   B _____ the floor.
      In   On

4. **A** Where's my dictionary?
   B _____ the filing cabinet.
      In   On

5. **A** Where's my ruler?
   B _____ the table.
      In   On

Listen and repeat. Then practice with a partner.

B **Look at the picture.** Match the words.

1. my book ———— on the desk
2. my eraser   in the notebook
3. my notebook   on the book
4. my pencil   on the paper
5. my paper   in the desk
6. my pen   on the chair

Talk with a partner. Act it out.

> **A** Where's my **book**?
> **B** **In the desk.**
> **A** Thanks.

3 Communicate

Talk with a partner. Complete the chart.

> **A** Where's my **pencil**?
> **B** **On the desk.**

Useful language
I don't know.

my pencil	*on the desk*
my book	
my paper	
my pen	

Lesson D Reading

1 Before you read

Talk about the picture.
What do you see?

2 Read

 SELF-STUDY AUDIO CD **Listen and read.**

Sue,

Have fun at school!
You need a pencil. The pencil is in the desk.
You need a notebook. The notebook is on
my computer. You need a dictionary. It's on
your chair. You need an eraser. It's on the
desk!

Love,
Mom

3 After you read

Read and match.

1

2

The pencil is
in the desk.

The notebook is
on the computer.

The dictionary is
on the chair.

The eraser is
on the desk.

3

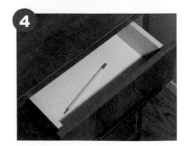

4

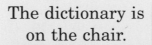

24   Unit 2

4 Picture dictionary Days of the week

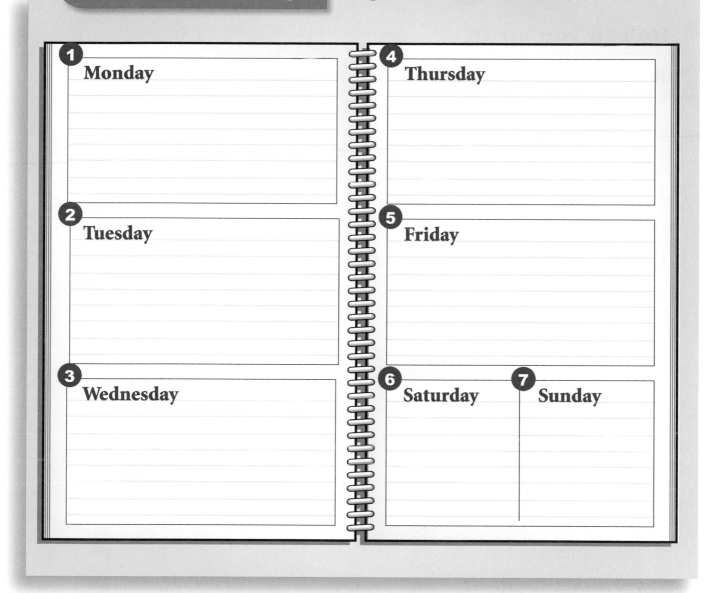

1 Monday

2 Tuesday

3 Wednesday

4 Thursday

5 Friday

6 Saturday

7 Sunday

 SELF-STUDY AUDIO CD

A 🔊 **Listen and repeat.** Look at the picture dictionary.

B Talk with a partner. Point and ask. Your partner answers.

> *A* What day is it?
> *B* **Monday.**

Lesson E *Writing*

1 Before you write

A Talk with a partner. Complete the words.

1. e r a s e <u>r</u>
2. d i c t i o n a r ___
3. p e ___
4. p e n c i ___
5. n o t e b o o ___

B Talk with a partner. Look at the picture. Write the words.

1. *dictionary*
2.
3.
4.
5.

2 Write

A Read the memo.

> # Welcome to South Side Adult School!
>
> The first day of school is Monday.
> Your teacher is Ms. Moreno.
> Your class is in Room 101.
> For class, you need:
>> a dictionary
>> a notebook
>> a pencil
>> a pen
>> an eraser

B Complete the memo. Write about yourself.

> The first day of school is _____ .
>
> My teacher is _____ .
>
> My class is in Room _____ .
>
> For class, I need _____ .
>
> I need _____ .
>
> I need _____ .
>
> I need _____ .

3 After you write

Talk with a partner. Share your writing.

Another view

1 Life-skills reading

MAIN STREET COMMUNITY SCHOOL JANUARY CLASS SCHEDULE

English 1	**Introduction to Computers**
TEACHER: Lynn Jones	TEACHER: Harry Dawson
ROOM: 12	ROOM: Computer Lab A
Tuesday and Thursday	Monday and Wednesday
10:00 a.m.–12:00 noon	1:00 p.m.–2:00 p.m.

A Read the sentences. Look at the class schedule.
Circle the answers.

1. English class is on ____ .
   a. Monday and Wednesday
   b. Tuesday and Thursday

2. Computer class is on ____ .
   a. Monday and Wednesday
   b. Tuesday and Thursday

3. English class is in ____ .
   a. Room 1
   b. Room 12

4. Computer class is in ____ .
   a. Lab A
   b. Lab B

B Talk with a partner.

Talk about your class schedule.

2 Fun with language

A Talk with a partner. What's in your classroom?
Check (✓).

☐ a book	☐ a chair	☐ a computer
☐ a desk	☐ a dictionary	☐ an eraser
☐ a notebook	☐ paper	☐ a pen
☐ a pencil	☐ a ruler	☐ a stapler

B Circle the words in the puzzle.

book	chair	computer	desk	dictionary	eraser
notebook	paper	pen	pencil	ruler	stapler

```
h  s  h  f  e  (b  o  o  k)  t  z  a
q  u  p  e  n  c  i  l  a  f  r  s
l  i  g  o  w  n  e  r  a  s  e  r
v  y  b  d  e  s  k  a  f  l  k  o
d  i  c  t  i  o  n  a  r  y  o  j
f  e  t  h  s  t  a  p  l  e  r  e
w  r  n  n  o  t  e  b  o  o  k  r
p  e  n  k  v  l  z  o  j  s  y  n
o  t  c  o  m  p  u  t  e  r  m  q
t  r  u  l  e  r  g  a  r  x  z  a
h  o  m  t  c  z  e  c  h  a  i  r
p  a  p  e  r  n  y  i  d  e  m  t
```

3 Wrap up

Complete the **Self-assessment** on page 142.

1 Listening

Read. Then listen and circle.

1. What's his first name?
   a. Maria
   b. Hassan ⟲

2. What's his last name?
   a. Ali
   b. Garcia

3. Where is he from?
   a. Mexico
   b. Somalia

4. When is his birthday?
   a. in August
   b. in October

5. Where's the notebook?
   a. on the desk
   b. on the chair

6. Where's the paper?
   a. in the notebook
   b. on the chair

Talk with a partner. Ask and answer.

2 Vocabulary

Write. Complete the story.

| book | Brazil | card | February | name | Tuesday |

Welcome, Luisa Ruiz!

Luisa is a new student. She is from _____*Brazil*_____ .
1

Her last _____ is Ruiz. Her birthday
2

is in _____ . In fact, her birthday is on
3

_____ . Happy birthday! Luisa needs a
4

_____ and an ID _____ .
5   6

Welcome, Luisa!

3 Grammar

A Complete the sentences.
Use *in* or *on*.

1. The dictionary is __*on*__ the desk.
2. The pen is _____ the notebook.
3. The book is _____ the chair.
4. The stapler is _____ the desk.

B Read and circle. Then write.

1. ___*His*___ name is Alberto.
   (His) Her
2. _____ name is Layla.
   His   Her
3. *A* What is _____ name?
        his   your
   B _____ name is Kim.
       My   Your

4 Pronunciation

A 🔊 Listen to the *a* sound and the *o* sound.

    a   **o**

name   phone

B 🔊 Listen and repeat.

a	name	day	say

o	phone	code	note

Talk with a partner. Say a word. Your partner points. Take turns.

C 🔊 Listen and check (✓).

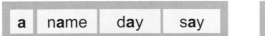

	a	o	a	o	a	o	a	o	a	o
1.	✓		2.		3.		4.		5.	

1 Talk about the picture

A Look at the picture. What do you see?

B Listen and point: daughter • father • grandfather
grandmother • mother • son

Friends and family

HAPPY BIRTHDAY, GRANDMA!

Gloria

2 Listening

SELF-STUDY
AUDIO CD **A** **Listen and repeat.**

1. daughter   2. father   3. grandfather
4. grandmother   5. mother   6. son

SELF-STUDY
AUDIO CD **B**  **Listen and circle.**

1 (a.)   b.

2 a.   b.

3 a.   b.

4 a.   b.

Listen again. Check your answers.

C Talk with a partner. Point to a picture
and ask. Your partner says the words.

Who's that?

The grandmother.

1 Vocabulary focus

💿 **Listen and repeat.**

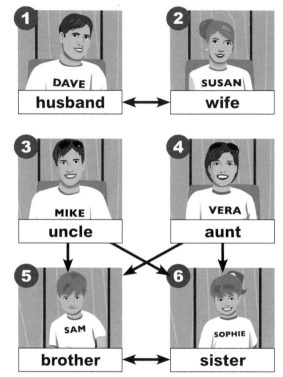

2 Practice

A Read and match.

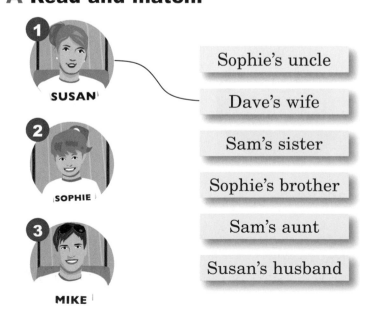

Sophie's uncle

Dave's wife

Sam's sister

Sophie's brother

Sam's aunt

Susan's husband

B 🔊 **Listen and repeat.** Then write.

aunt	brother	husband	sister	uncle	wife

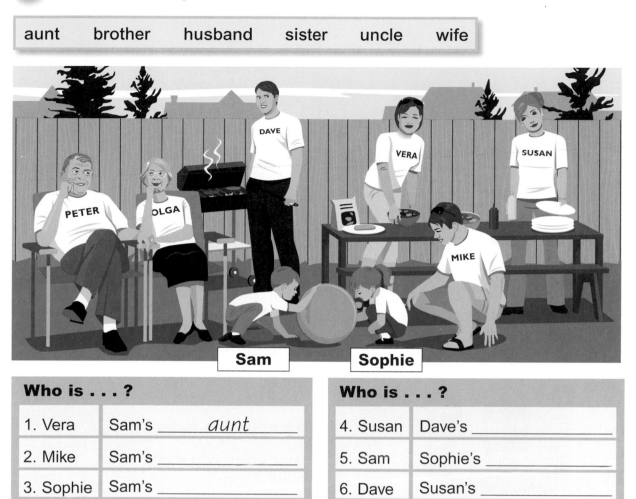

Who is . . . ?

1. Vera	Sam's _____*aunt*_____
2. Mike	Sam's _____
3. Sophie	Sam's _____

Who is . . . ?

4. Susan	Dave's _____
5. Sam	Sophie's _____
6. Dave	Susan's _____

Talk with a partner. Ask and answer.

A Who is **Vera**?
B **Sam's aunt.**

3 Communicate

Complete the chart about your family.
Then talk with a partner.

Name	Family member
Habib	brother

A Who is **Habib**?
B My **brother**.

Do you have a sister?

1 Grammar focus: *Do you have . . . ?*

Do you have a sister?	Yes,	I we	do.	No,	I we	don't.

don't = do not

2 Practice

A Read and circle. Then write.

1

A Do you have a brother?

B _____*Yes, I do.*_____

(Yes, I do.)   No, I don't.

2

A Do you have a sister?

B _____

Yes, we do.   No, we don't.

3

A Do you have a son?

B _____

Yes, I do.   No, I don't.

4

A Do you have a daughter?

B _____

Yes, we do.   No, we don't.

5

A Do you have a wife?

B _____

Yes, I do.   No, I don't.

🔊 **Listen and repeat.** Then practice with a partner.

B  Listen and repeat. Then write.

Ken, Danny, and me

Me, Grandma Rose, and Diana

Do you have a . . . ?

1. sister	*yes*	4. son	
2. brother		5. daughter	
3. husband		6. grandmother	

Talk with a partner. Ask and answer.

> **A** Do you have **a sister**?
> **B** **Yes**, I **do**.
> **A** What's **her** name?
> **B** **Diana.**

3 Communicate

Talk with your classmates. Complete the chart.

Do you have a . . . ?	Dinh					
	Yes	No	Yes	No	Yes	No
son		✓				
daughter	✓					
sister	✓					
brother	✓					

Lesson D Reading

1 Before you read

Talk about the picture.
What do you see?

2 Read

SELF-STUDY AUDIO CD   **Listen and read.**

My Family

My name is Gloria. This is my family. This is my mother. Her name is Natalia. It is her birthday. This is my father. His name is Enrico. This is my husband, Luis. This is our daughter, Lisa. This is our son, Tony. I love my family!

3 After you read

Read and circle. Then write.

1. Luis is Gloria's _____*husband*_____ .
   father (husband)
2. Natalia is Gloria's _____ .
   daughter   mother
3. Tony is Gloria's _____ .
   brother   son
4. Enrico is Gloria's _____ .
   father   mother
5. Lisa is Gloria's _____ .
   sister   daughter

1 baby

2 girl

3 boy

4 teenager

5 woman

6 man

A 🔊 **Listen and repeat.** Look at the picture dictionary.

B **Talk with a partner.** Say a word. Your partner points to the picture.

> *A* Show me the **man**.
> *B* Here's the **man**.

1 Before you write

A Talk with a partner. Complete the words.

Frank's Family

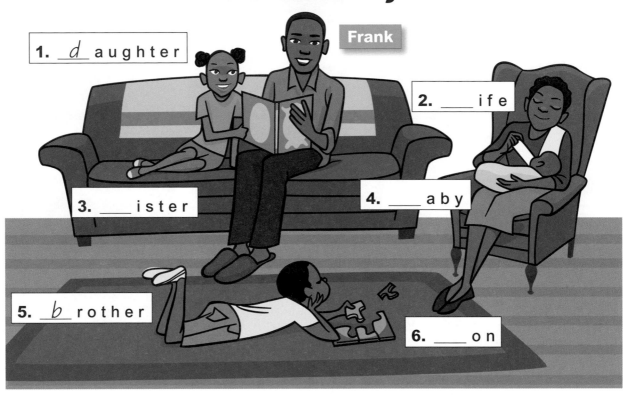

1. _d_ a u g h t e r

Frank

2. ____ i f e

3. ____ i s t e r

4. ____ a b y

5. _b_ r o t h e r

6. ____ o n

B Talk with a partner. Look at the picture. Complete the story.

My Wonderful Family

My name is Frank. This is my family. This is my _____*wife*_____ ,
                                                        1
Marie. This is our _____ . His name is Patrick. This is
                          2
our _____ . Her name is Annie. This is our new
            3
_____ , Jason. He is a boy. Patrick is his _____ .
        4   5
Annie is his _____ . I have a wonderful family!
                    6

---

2 Write

A Draw a picture of your family.

B Write about your picture.

daughter	father	husband	mother	son	wife

My Wonderful Family

My name is _____ . This is my family.

This is my _____ . _____ name is _____ .
                                                  His   Her

This is my _____ . _____ name is _____ .
                                                  His   Her

This is my _____ . _____ name is _____ .
                                                  His   Her

This is my _____ . _____ name is _____ .
                                                  His   Her

I love my family!

3 After you write

Talk with a partner. Share your writing.

Another view

1 Life-skills reading

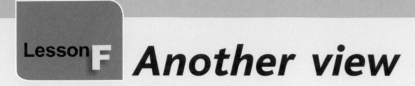

PROPERTY MANAGEMENT COMPANY
230 CENTRAL AVENUE
PHILADELPHIA, PA 19019
(215) 555-1863

HOUSING APPLICATION

DIRECTIONS: Complete the form. Please print.

What is your name? _Ali Azari_

Who will live with you in the house?

NAME	RELATIONSHIP
Shohreh Azari	wife
Azam Javadi	mother
Omid Azari	son
Navid Azari	son
Fatima Azari	daughter
Leila Azari	daughter
Soraya Azari	daughter

A **Read the questions.** Look at the housing application. Circle the answers.

1. Who is Shohreh Azari?
   a. Ali's daughter
   b. Ali's wife

2. Who is Soraya Azari?
   a. Ali's daughter
   b. Ali's mother

3. Who is Azam Javadi?
   a. Ali's mother
   b. Ali's wife

4. Who is Omid Azari?
   a. Ali's brother
   b. Ali's son

B **Talk with a partner.**

Who lives in your house?

2 Fun with language

A **Complete the chart.**

an aunt	a girl	a sister
a baby	a grandfather	a son
a boy	a grandmother	a teenager
a brother	a husband	an uncle
a daughter	a man	a wife
a father	a mother	a woman

Male	Female	Male or female
	an aunt	

Talk with a partner. Compare your answers.

B **Write about yourself.** Use the words from 2A.

I am _____ , _____ ,

and _____ .

Talk with a partner. Write about your partner.

My partner is _____ , _____ ,

and _____ .

3 Wrap up

Complete the **Self-assessment** on page 143.

Lesson A *Get ready*

1 Talk about the picture

A Look at the picture. What do you see?

B 💿 Listen and point: doctor • doctor's office • medicine
nurse • patient

Dr. Brown's Office

Mario

Tony

2 Listening

  A **Listen and repeat.**

1. doctor **2.** doctor's office **3.** medicine **4.** nurse **5.** patient

  B  **Listen and circle.**

1 a.  (b.)

2 a.  b.

3 a.  b.

4 a.  b.

Listen again. Check your answers.

C Talk with a partner. Point to a picture. Your partner says the word.

Nurse.

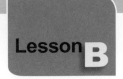
Parts of the body

1 Vocabulary focus

💿 **Listen and repeat.**

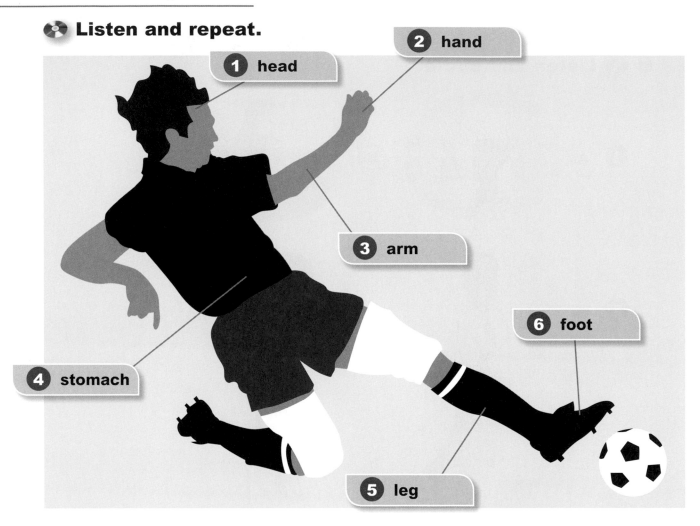

1 head
2 hand
3 arm
4 stomach
5 leg
6 foot

2 Practice

A Read and match.

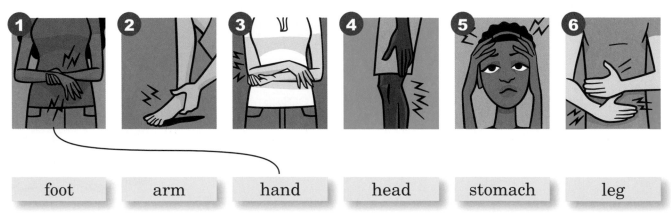

| foot | arm | hand | head | stomach | leg |

B 🔊 **Listen and repeat.** Then write.

arm	foot	hand	head	leg	stomach

What hurts?

1. My _____*hand*_____ .   4. My _____ .
2. My _____ .   5. My _____ .
3. My _____ .   6. My _____ .

Talk with a partner. Act it out. Ask and answer.

> *A* What's the matter?
> *B* My **hand** hurts.

3 Communicate

Talk with a partner.
Act it out. Ask and answer.

What's the matter?   My head hurts.

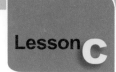

My feet hurt.

1 Grammar focus: *1 hand, 2 hands*

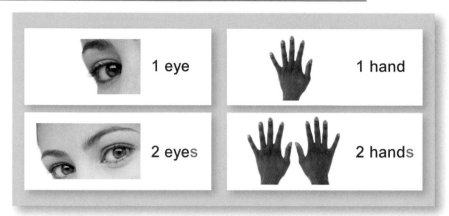

1 eye	1 hand	1 foot
2 eyes	2 hands	2 feet

2 Practice

A Read and circle. Then write.

A What hurts?

B My ___*hands*___ .

         hand (hands)

A What hurts?

B My _____ .

         eye   eyes

A What hurts?

B My _____ .

         arm   arms

A What hurts?

B My _____ .

         foot   feet

A What hurts?

B My _____ .

         leg   legs

A What hurts?

B My _____ .

         hand   hands

Listen and repeat. Then practice with a partner.

B 🔊 Listen and repeat.

1 legs

2 hand

3 stomach

4 feet

5 eyes

6 head

Talk with a partner. Act it out. Ask and answer.

A What hurts?
B My **legs**.
A Oh, I'm sorry.

3 Communicate

Talk with your classmates.
Complete the chart.

A What hurts, **Sasha**?
B My **head**.

Name	What hurts?
Sasha	head

Lesson D Reading

1 Before you read

Talk about the picture.
What do you see?

2 Read

 SELF-STUDY AUDIO CD **Listen and read.**

At the Doctor's Office

Tony and Mario are at the doctor's office. They are patients. Tony's leg hurts. His head hurts, too. Mario's arm hurts. His hands hurt, too. Tony and Mario are not happy. It is not a good day.

3 After you read

Read the sentences. Check (✓) the names.

	Tony	Mario
His arm hurts.		✓
His head hurts.		
His leg hurts.		
His hands hurt.		
He is not happy.		

4 *Picture dictionary* Health problems

1	2	3
a cold	a fever	a headache
4	5	6
a sore throat	a stomachache	a toothache

 SELF-STUDY AUDIO CD **A** ✷ **Listen and repeat.** Look at the picture dictionary.

B Talk with a partner. Act it out. Ask and answer questions.

> *A* What's the matter?
> *B* I have **a cold**.

1 Before you write

Talk with a partner. Check (✓) the reason for the visit.

1 Name: *Regina*
Reason for visit:

- [ ] cold
- [ ] fever
- [ ] headache
- [ ] sore throat
- [ ] stomachache
- [✓] toothache

2 Name: *Isaac*
Reason for visit:

- [ ] cold
- [ ] fever
- [ ] headache
- [ ] sore throat
- [ ] stomachache
- [ ] toothache

3 Name: *Joe*
Reason for visit:

- [ ] cold
- [ ] fever
- [ ] headache
- [ ] sore throat
- [ ] stomachache
- [ ] toothache

4 Name: *Esperanza*
Reason for visit:

- [ ] cold
- [ ] fever
- [ ] headache
- [ ] sore throat
- [ ] stomachache
- [ ] toothache

5 Name: *James*
Reason for visit:

- [ ] cold
- [ ] fever
- [ ] headache
- [ ] sore throat
- [ ] stomachache
- [ ] toothache

6 Name: *Sue*
Reason for visit:

- [ ] cold
- [ ] fever
- [ ] headache
- [ ] sore throat
- [ ] stomachache
- [ ] toothache

2 Write

A **Talk with a partner.** Complete the words.

1. s _o_ re thr _o_ at
2. c ___ l d
3. s t ___ m a c h a c h e
4. h ___ a d a c h e
5. f ___ v e r
6. t ___ o t h a c h e

B **Look at page 52.** Then complete the patient sign-in sheet.

☤ Patient Sign-In Sheet

Name of Patient	Reason for Visit
Regina	I have a ___toothache___ .
Isaac	I have a _____ .
Joe	I have a _____ .
Esperanza	I have a _____ .
James	I have a _____ .
Sue	I have a _____ .

3 After you write

Talk with a partner. Share your writing.

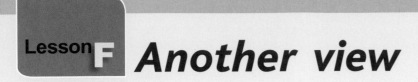

1 Life-skills reading

24 tablets

Colds Away

For relief of colds, headaches, and fevers

Do not use after December 2012.

A Read the sentences. Look at the label. Circle *Yes* or *No*.

1. This medicine is for a sore throat.
   a. Yes
   b. No

2. This medicine is for a headache.
   a. Yes
   b. No

3. This medicine is for a cold.
   a. Yes
   b. No

4. This medicine is for a stomachache.
   a. Yes
   b. No

B Talk with a partner.

What is this medicine for?

2 Fun with language

A Complete the chart. How many?

	The monster	You
heads	2	1
eyes		
ears		
arms		
legs		
feet		

Talk with a partner. Compare your answers.

B Write the missing letters.

p a t _*i*_ e n t
    1

f _ _ _ v e r
 2

s t o _ _ _ a c h
   3

_ _ _ u r s e
 4

t o o t h a _ _ _ h e
     5

_ _ _ o c t o r
 6

o f f _ _ _ c e
   7

_ _ _ y e
 8

Write the letters. Make a word.

_____ _____ _____ _*i*_ _____ _____ _____ _____
 3   2   6   1   5   7   4   8

3 Wrap up

Complete the **Self-assessment** on page 144.

1 Listening

Read. Then listen and circle.

1. Who is Sonya?
   a. Tom's aunt
   b. Tom's brother

2. Who is David?
   a. Tom's aunt
   b. Tom's brother

3. Who is Tina?
   a. Ray's sister
   b. Ray's wife

4. Who is Jay?
   a. Barbara's son
   b. Barbara's brother

5. What hurts?
   a. her hand
   b. her head

6. What hurts?
   a. his leg
   b. his foot

Talk with a partner. Ask and answer.

2 Vocabulary

Write. Complete the story.

| cold | doctor's office | medicine | patients | stomach |

A Visit to the Doctor

Marisa and her family are at the _doctor's office_ .
                                        1
They are _____ . Peter is Marisa's son. His
              2
_____ hurts. Antonia is Marisa's daughter. She has
        3
a _____ . They need _____ . Marisa
        4   5
isn't happy. She has a headache!

3 Grammar

A Read and circle. Then write.

1. What hurts? His ___leg___ .
   ((leg)) legs
2. What hurts? His _____ .
   arm   arms
3. What hurts? Her _____ .
   hand   hands
4. What hurts? Her _____ .
   foot   feet

B Complete the sentences. Use *do* or *don't*.

A ___Do___ you have a daughter?
1

B Yes, we _____ .
2

A _____ you have a son?
3

B Yes, we _____ .
4

A _____ you have a sister?
5

B No, I _____ .
6

4 Pronunciation

A 💿 Listen to the *e* sound, the *i* sound, and the *u* sound.

e	i	u
read	five	June

B 💿 Listen and repeat.

e	read	need		i	five	write		u	June	rule

Talk with a partner. Say a word. Your partner points. Take turns.

C 💿 Listen and check (✓).

	e	i	u		e	i	u		e	i	u		e	i	u		e	i	u
1.		✓		2.				3.				4.				5.			

Lesson A *Get ready*

1 Talk about the picture

A Look at the picture. What do you see?

B 💿 Listen and point: bank • library • restaurant
school • street • supermarket

2 Listening

  A 🔊 **Listen and repeat.**

1. bank   2. library   3. restaurant
4. school   5. street   6. supermarket

B 🔊 **Listen and circle.**

1   (a.)    b.

2   a.    b.

3   a.    b.

4   a.    b.

Listen again. Check your answers.

C **Talk with a partner.** Point to a picture.
Your partner says the word.

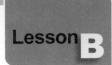

Lesson B · *Places around town*

1 Vocabulary focus

 Listen and repeat.

1 FAMILY DRUGSTORE Rx

drugstore

2 SOUTH SIDE HOSPITAL · AMBULANCE

hospital

3 BUBBLES LAUNDROMAT

laundromat

4 CITY POST OFFICE

post office

5 CENTRAL THEATER YOUR TOWN 2:00, 5:00, 8:00

movie theater

6 FIRST STREET SENIOR CENTER

senior center

2 Practice

A Read and match.

1 LIFE STORY 7:30

2 Rx

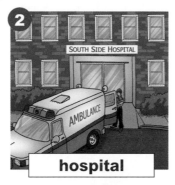

3

post office

movie theater

drugstore

laundromat

hospital

senior center

4

5

6

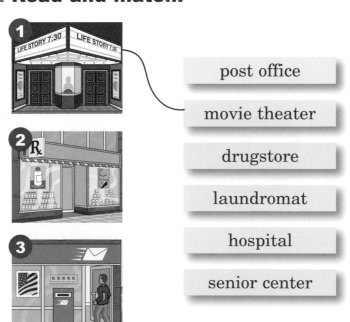

B  Listen and repeat. Then write.

drugstore	hospital	laundromat
movie theater	post office	senior center

1  Minh

2  Alan

3  Mr. Lopez

4  Paula

5  Jackie

6  Isabel

Name	Place		Name	Place
1. Minh	*movie theater*		4. Paula	
2. Alan			5. Jackie	
3. Mr. Lopez			6. Isabel	

Talk with a partner. Ask and answer.

A Where's **Minh**?
B At the **movie theater**.

3 Communicate

Work in a group. Play a game.
Ask and guess.

A Where is **she**?
B At the **movie theater**?
C Right!

1 Grammar focus: *on, next to, across from, between*

Where's the school?

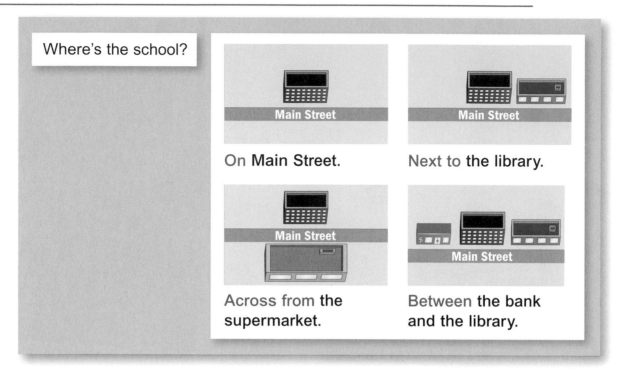

On Main Street.

Next to the library.

Across from the supermarket.

Between the bank and the library.

2 Practice

A Read and circle. Then write.

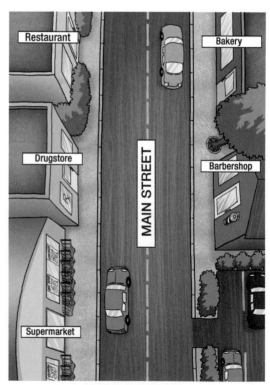

1. **A** Where's the drugstore?

   B _____*Next to*_____ the supermarket.

   (Next to)   Across from

2. **A** Where's the supermarket?

   B _____ Main Street.

   Across from   On

3. **A** Where's the restaurant?

   B _____ the drugstore.

   Between   Next to

4. **A** Where's the bakery?

   B _____ the restaurant.

   Next to   Across from

5. **A** Where's the barbershop?

   B _____ the bakery.

   On   Next to

💿 **Listen and repeat.** Then practice with a partner.

B 🔊 Listen and repeat.

next to

across from

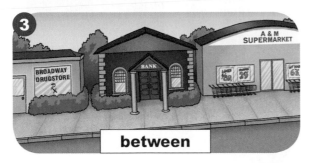

between

on

next to

across from

Talk with a partner. Ask and answer.

> **A** Excuse me. Where's the **bank**?
> **B** **Next to the supermarket.**
> **A** Thanks.

3 Communicate

Talk with a partner. Play a game.
Ask and guess.

> **A** Where are you?
> **B** **Next to the supermarket.**
> **A** At the **bank**?
> **B** Right.

Lesson D Reading

1 Before you read

Talk about the picture.
What do you see?

2 Read

 SELF-STUDY AUDIO CD

🔊 **Listen and read.**

Notice from Riverside Library

Come and visit Riverside Library. The new library opens today. The library is on Main Street. It is across from Riverside Adult School. It is next to K and P Supermarket. It is between K and P Supermarket and Rosie's Restaurant. The library is open from 9:00 to 5:00, Monday, Wednesday, and Friday.

3 After you read

Complete the map. Share your map with a partner.

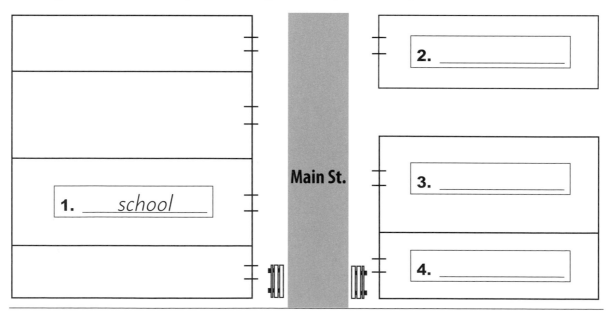

Main St.

1. _____school_____

2. _____

3. _____

4. _____

4 *Picture dictionary* Transportation

by bicycle

by bus

by car

by taxi

by train

on foot

A **Listen and repeat.** Look at the picture dictionary.

B **Talk with your classmates.** Complete the chart.

A **Ben,** how do you get to school?
B **By car.**

Name	Transportation
Ben	by car

Lesson E Writing

1 Before you write

A Talk with a partner. Complete the words.

1. s u p e r m a r _k_ e t
2. d r u g ___ t o r e
3. p o s t o f ___ i c e
4. r e s ___ a u r a n t
5. l i ___ r a r y
6. s ___ h o o l

B Talk with a partner. Look at the map. Complete the story.

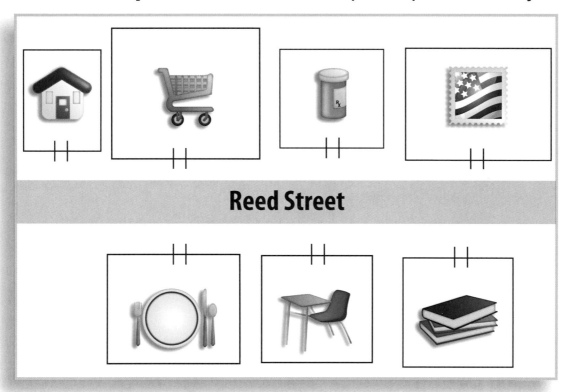

Reed Street

Donna lives on Reed _____*Street*_____ . She lives next to a big
                                  1

__*supermarket*__ . The supermarket is next to a _____ .
       2   3

A _____ is across from the supermarket. A
            4

_____ _____ is on Reed Street, too. It is across from the
            5

_____ . A _____ is between the restaurant
       6   7

and the library.

66   Unit 5

2 Write

A Draw a map of your street.

B Write about your street.

My Street

I live on _____ .

_____ is next to a _____ .

_____ is across from _____ .

_____ is between the _____

and the _____ .

3 After you write

Listen to your partner. Draw your partner's street.

1 Life-skills reading

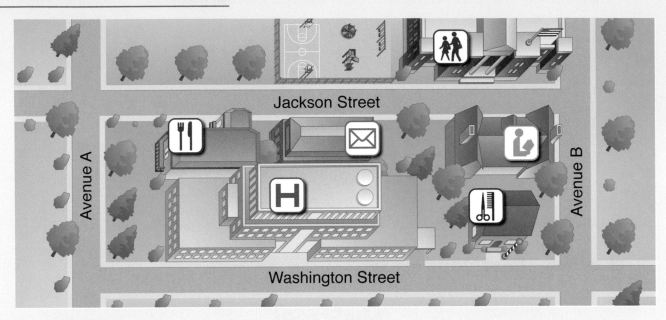

Jackson Street

Avenue A

Avenue B

Washington Street

A Read the sentences. Look at the map. Circle the answers.

1. The hospital is _____ .
   a. on Jackson Street
   b. on Washington Street

2. The post office is _____ .
   a. next to the barbershop
   b. next to the restaurant

3. The post office is _____ .
   a. between the restaurant and the library
   b. across from the library

4. The hospital is _____ .
   a. across from the school
   b. next to the barbershop

B Talk with a partner.

Where is the library?
Where is the school?

2 Fun with language

A Read and match.

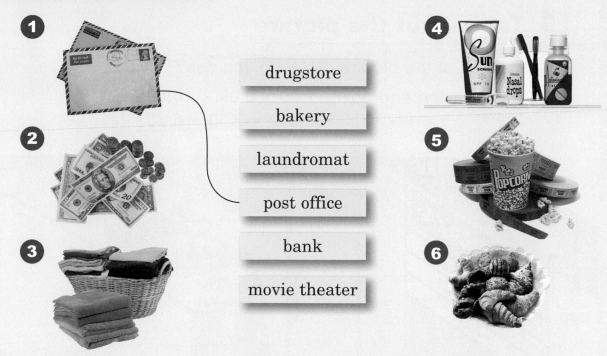

1 — post office

drugstore	**4**
bakery	
laundromat	**5**
post office	
bank	**6**
movie theater	

Talk with a partner. Check your answers.

B Circle the words in the puzzle.

bicycle	bus	car	foot	taxi	train

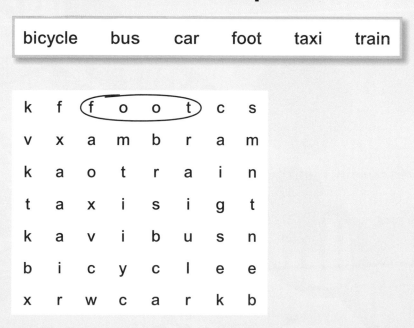

```
k  f  f  o  o  t  c  s
v  x  a  m  b  r  a  m
k  a  o  t  r  a  i  n
t  a  x  i  s  i  g  t
k  a  v  i  b  u  s  n
b  i  c  y  c  l  e  e
x  r  w  c  a  r  k  b
```

3 Wrap up

Complete the **Self-assessment** on page 145.

Lesson A Get ready

Time

1 Talk about the picture

A Look at the picture. What do you see?

B Listen and point: 7:00 • 9:00 • 10:00
10:30 • 2:30 • 6:30

2 Listening

SELF-STUDY
AUDIO CD

A 💿 **Listen and repeat.**

1. 7:00   **2.** 9:00   **3.** 10:00
4. 10:30   **5.** 2:30   **6.** 6:30

SELF-STUDY
AUDIO CD

B 💿 **Listen and circle.**

1   a.    b.

2   a.    b.

3   a.    b.

4   a.    b.

Listen again. Check your answers.

C **Talk with a partner.** Point to a picture and ask. Your partner says the time.

What time is it?   It's 10:00.

Useful language
Say times like this.
3:00 = three o'clock
6:30 = six-thirty

1 Vocabulary focus

🔘 Listen and repeat.

SEPTEMBER

			1	2	3	4
5	6 **1 appointment** 1:30	7	8 **2 meeting**	9 3:30	10	11
12	13 **3 class**	14 page 6 8:30	15	16 **4 movie**	17 7:30	18
19	20	21	22	23	24	25
26 **5 party** 5:00	27	28 **6 program**	29 4:30	30		

2 Practice

A Read and match.

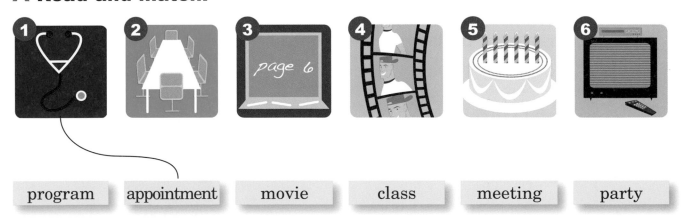

program   appointment   movie   class   meeting   party

Town Barbershop

APPOINTMENT INFO:

Day & Time: *Friday 1:30*

Haircut with: *Nick*

English Class Friday 8:30

4:30 — **Friday**

3 One Life, One Love
1 hour

5 Dinosaurs
30 minutes

7 Afternoon Special
1 hour

RIVERSIDE SCHOOL

PTA MEETING
SATURDAY 3:00

ATTACK FROM VENUS!!

NOW PLAYING: SATURDAY 7:00 p.m.

You're Invited!

Gina's Birthday Party
Saturday 5:00

Event	Time	Day
appointment	1:30	Friday
program		
movie		

Event	Time	Day
class		
party		
meeting		

Talk with a partner. Ask and answer.

A What time is the **appointment**?
B At **1:30** on **Friday**.

3 Communicate

Complete the chart. Then talk with your classmates.

Event	Time	Day
movie	9:00	Saturday
program		
party		

A What time is the **movie**?
B At **9:00** on **Saturday**.

Is your class at 11:00?

1 Grammar focus: Yes/No questions with be

Is	your class	at 11:00?

Yes,	it is.
No,	it isn't.

isn't = is not

2 Practice

A Read and circle. Then write.

1

Class	Time	
English	11:00	

A Is your class at 11:00?

B _____Yes, it is._____

(Yes, it is.)   No, it isn't.

2

Appointment with: __Dr. Martin__

Patient: __Kamal Ali__

When: __November 7, 1:30__

A Is your appointment at 12:30?

B _____

Yes, it is.   No, it isn't.

3

≫ The Paramount Concert Hall ≪

Toni Tucker

Tonight Only! 8:30 p.m.

A Is your concert at 8:00?

B _____

Yes, it is.   No, it isn't.

4

THE LOST CLUES 6:00

A Is your movie at 6:00?

B _____

Yes, it is.   No, it isn't.

5

SAMMY'S BIRTHDAY PARTY 4:00

A Is your party at 4:00?

B _____

Yes, it is.   No, it isn't.

6

Singing Stars

7:00   Who wins? Final three singers.

A Is your program at 7:30?

B _____

Yes, it is.   No, it isn't.

Listen and repeat. Then practice with a partner.

B Read and match.

```
April
 2 Monday                          6 Friday
   3:30 – Doctor's appointment       7:30 – Birthday party

 3 Tuesday                         7 Saturday
   6:30 – English class              9:00 – Concert – Salsa music

 4 Wednesday                       8 Sunday
   12:00 – Meeting at work

 5 Thursday
   8:00 – Movie with my sister
```

1. appointment   seven-thirty
2. class   six-thirty
3. meeting   three-thirty
4. movie   nine o'clock
5. party   twelve o'clock
6. concert   eight o'clock

Talk with a partner. Ask and answer.

> **A** Is your **appointment** on **Monday**?
> **B** Yes, it is.
> **A** Is your **appointment** at **7:00**?
> **B** No, it isn't. It's at 3:30.

3 Communicate

Write events on the calendar. Then talk with a partner.

Monday	Tuesday	Wednesday	Thursday	Friday
5:00 – Class				

> **A** Is your **class** on **Monday**?
> **B** Yes, it is.
> **A** Is your **class** at **4:00**?
> **B** No, it isn't. It's at 5:00.

1 Before you read

Talk about the picture.
What do you see?

2 Read

  Listen and read.

Teresa's Day

Teresa is busy today. Her meeting with her friend Joan is at 10:00. Her doctor's appointment is at 1:00. Her favorite TV program is at 4:30. Her class is at 6:30. Her uncle's birthday party is at 6:30, too. Oh, no! What will she do?

3 After you read

Write the answers.

1. What time is Teresa's meeting? *At 10:00.*
2. What time is Teresa's TV program? _____
3. What time is Teresa's class? _____
4. Is Teresa's appointment at 4:00? _____
5. Is her party at 6:30? _____

4 Picture dictionary Times of the day

in the morning

in the afternoon

in the evening

at night

at midnight

at noon

A 🔊 **Listen and repeat.** Look at the picture dictionary.

B **Talk with a partner.** Complete the chart.
Check (✓) the time of the day.

> *A* It's **12:00 p.m.**
> *B* At noon?
> *A* Right.

Useful language
a.m. = from midnight to noon
p.m. = from noon to midnight

	In the morning	In the afternoon	In the evening	At noon	At midnight
12:00 p.m.				✓	
3:00 p.m.					
6:00 a.m.					
12:00 a.m.					
6:00 p.m.					

Time   77

Lesson E Writing

1 Before you write

A Talk with a partner. Complete the words.

1. m o v _i_ _e_
2. c l a ___ ___
3. a p p ___ ___ n t m e n t
4. p ___ ___ t y
5. p ___ ___ g r a m
6. m ___ ___ t i n g

B Talk with a partner. Look at the memo.

MEMO

Time	Event
8:00 a.m.	meeting
12:00 p.m.	doctor's appointment
1:30 p.m.	class
6:00 p.m.	party
8:00 p.m.	TV program

My Busy Day

Today is a busy day. My ___meeting___ at my daughter's school
₁

is at 8:00 in the morning. Then my doctor's _____ is at
₂

noon. My English _____ is at 1:30. What time is my son's
₃

class _____ ? Oh, yes. At 6:00 in the evening. Dinner with
₄

my family is at 7:00. And my favorite TV _____ is at 8:00
₅

at night. It's a very busy day.

2 Write

A Complete the memo. Write four times. Write four events.

MEMO

Time   Event
_____   _____
_____   _____
_____   _____
_____   _____

B Write about your day.

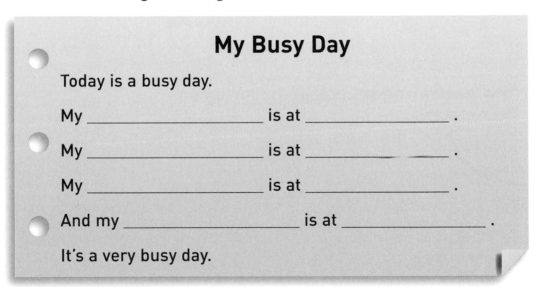

My Busy Day

Today is a busy day.

My _____ is at _____ .

My _____ is at _____ .

My _____ is at _____ .

And my _____ is at _____ .

It's a very busy day.

3 After you write

Talk with a partner. Share your writing.

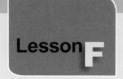
1 Life-skills reading

It's a party!

Lily is 50! It's her surprise party!

When: *Saturday, October 2*

What time: *8:00 p.m.*

Where: *Katya and Alex's house*
874 Lake Road

RSVP: *555-6188*

A Read the sentences. Look at the invitation.
Circle the answers.

1. It's a party for ____ .
   a. Katya and Alex
   b. Lily

2. The party is ____ .
   a. in the morning
   b. at night

3. The party is at ____ .
   a. 2:00
   b. 8:00

4. The party is on ____ .
   a. Saturday
   b. Sunday

B Talk with a partner about the party.

Tell the day, the time, and the place.

2 Fun with language

A Write times on the clocks.

Talk with a partner. Listen and write your partner's times.

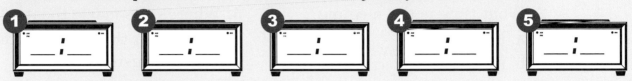

> **A** What time is it?
> **B** It's **10:00**.

B Write the missing letters.

_d_ a y
1

e v e n ___ n g
2

m o r n i n ___
3

___ o v i e
4

n o o ___
5

a f ___ e r n o o n
6

n i g ___ t
7

a p p o ___ n t m e n t
8

What time is it? Write the letters below.

_____ _____ _d_ _____ _____ _____ _____ _____
4   8   1   5   2   3   7   6

3 Wrap up

Complete the **Self-assessment** on page 146.

1 Listening

🔵 **Read.** Then listen and circle.

1. Is the meeting on Friday?
   (a.) Yes, it is.
   b. No, it isn't.

2. What time is the meeting?
   a. at 2:30
   b. at 10:30

3. What time is the appointment?
   a. at 2:00
   b. at 4:00

4. Where's the school?
   a. next to the bank
   b. across from the bank

5. Where's the movie theater?
   a. between the supermarket and
      the drugstore
   b. next to the supermarket

6. Is the movie at 7:30?
   a. Yes, it is.
   b. No, it isn't.

Talk with a partner. Ask and answer.

2 Vocabulary

Write. Complete the story.

afternoon	class	8:30	hospital	meeting

Tan's Day

Tan's English _____*class*_____ is at _____
in the morning. His _____ is at 1:00 p.m. in the
_____ . The meeting is at the _____ ,
next to the school. It's a busy day.

3 Grammar

A Read and circle. Then write.

1. The library is ___across from___ the bank.
   on   (across from)

2. The post office is _____ the bank and the school.
   next to   between

3. The restaurant is _____ Main Street.
   on   between

4. The hospital is _____ the supermarket.
   across from   between

B Read the memo and answer. Write *Yes, it is* or *No, it isn't*.

1. Is the party at 6:00?
   ___No, it isn't___ .

2. Is the class at 9:00?

   _____ .

3. Is the meeting in the morning?

   _____ .

4. Is the appointment in the afternoon?

   _____ .

Morning
9:00 class
Afternoon
2:00 – meeting with Ms. Morales
4:30 – appointment with Dr. Morgan
Evening
6:30 – party at senior center

4 Pronunciation

A 💿 **Listen** to the *a* sound and the *o* sound.

a   o
at   on

B 💿 **Listen and repeat.**

| a | at | class | map |

| o | on | clock | not |

Talk with a partner. Say a word. Your partner points. Take turns.

C 💿 **Listen and check (✓).**

	a	o		a	o		a	o		a	o		a	o
1.		✓	2.			3.			4.			5.		

Shopping

1 Talk about the picture

A Look at the picture. What do you see?

B 🔊 Listen and point: a dress • pants • a shirt
shoes • socks • a T-shirt

SUMMER SALE!

THE CLOTHES PLACE

$39.99

$27.00

$19.00

$1.99

$24.99

$10.99

Rose

Samuel

2 Listening

A  **Listen and repeat.**

1. a dress   2. pants   3. a shirt
4. shoes   5. socks   6. a T-shirt

B **Listen and circle.**

1 (a.)    b.

2 a.    b.

3 a.    b.

4 a.    b.

A dress.

Listen again. Check your answers.

C Talk with a partner. Point to a picture.
Your partner says the word.

1 Vocabulary focus

Listen and repeat.

Back-to-School SALE!

1. a tie $10.00
2. a blouse $19.99
3. a sweater $29.00
4. a skirt $24.99
5. a jacket $89.99
6. a raincoat $39.99

2 Practice

A Read and match.

| a tie | a blouse | a jacket | a skirt | a raincoat | a sweater |

B 🔊 **Listen and repeat.** Then write.

blouse	jacket	raincoat	skirt	sweater	tie

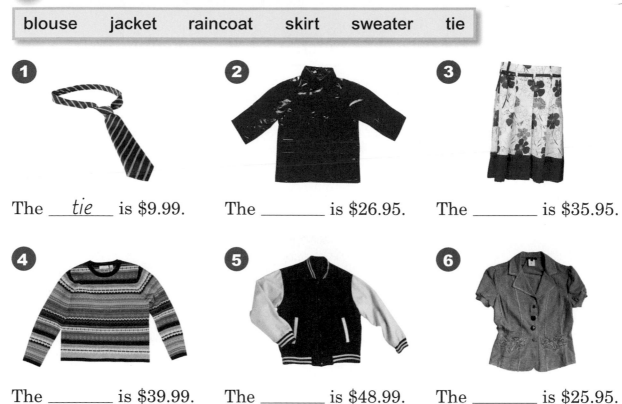

1

The _tie_ is $9.99.

2

The _____ is $26.95.

3

The _____ is $35.95.

4

The _____ is $39.99.

5

The _____ is $48.99.

6

The _____ is $25.95.

Talk with a partner. Ask and answer.

A How much is the **tie**?
B **$9.99.**

3 Communicate

Write prices. Your partner asks the price. You answer.

$ _24.99_ $ _____ $ _____ $ _____ $ _____

A How much is the **skirt**?
B **$24.99.**

How much are the shoes?

1 Grammar focus: *How much is? / How much are?*

How much	is	the shirt?	$15.99.
	are	the shoes?	$68.95.

2 Practice

A Read and circle. Then write.

1. **A** How much ___are___ the pants?
   is (are)
   B $24.99.

2. **A** How much _____ the skirt?
   is   are
   B $18.99.

3. **A** How much _____ the raincoat?
   is   are
   B $16.95.

4. **A** How much _____ the shoes?
   is   are
   B $58.99.

5. **A** How much _____ the sweater?
   is   are
   B $31.99.

6. **A** How much _____ the socks?
   is   are
   B $5.95.

💿 **Listen and repeat.** Then practice with a partner.

B 💿 **Listen and repeat.** Then write.

1. T-shirt *$2.00*
2. shoes
3. jacket
4. sweater
5. raincoat
6. pants
7. socks
8. blouse

Talk with a partner. Ask and answer.

A How much **is the T-shirt**?
B **$2.00.**
A **$2.00?** Thanks.

A How much **are the shoes**?
B **$3.00.**
A **$3.00?** Thanks.

3 Communicate

Write prices. Your partner asks the price. You answer.

$ ___5.00___ $ _____ $ _____ $ _____ $ _____

A How much **are the socks**?
B **$5.00.**

Lesson D Reading

1 Before you read

Talk about the picture.
What do you see?

SUMMER SALE!

$37.99 $24.99

$49.99 $39.99

$35.99 $19.99

2 Read

 SELF-STUDY AUDIO CD **Listen and read.**

TO: Patty <pthompson@cup.org>
FROM: Rose <roseV@cup.org>
Subject: Shopping
Hi Patty,
This morning, Samuel and I are going to The Clothes Place. Samuel needs blue pants. He needs a tie, too. I need a red dress and black shoes. Dresses are on sale. They're $39.99. Shoes are on sale, too. They're $19.99. That's good.
Call you later,
Rose

3 After you read

Read and match.

1

2

Samuel needs blue pants.

Samuel needs a tie.

Dresses are on sale.

Shoes are on sale.

3

4

90 Unit 7

4 Picture dictionary Colors

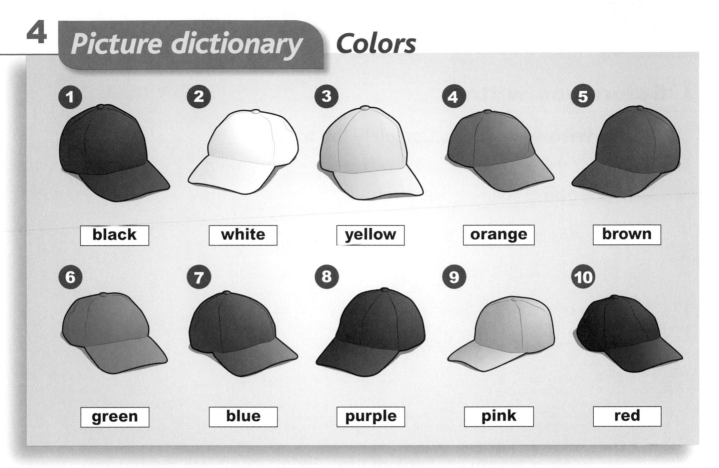

| 1 black | 2 white | 3 yellow | 4 orange | 5 brown |
| 6 green | 7 blue | 8 purple | 9 pink | 10 red |

SELF-STUDY AUDIO CD **A** 🔊 **Listen and repeat.** Look at the picture dictionary.

B Talk with a partner. Look around your classroom.
Ask and answer.

> *A* What color is **her sweater**?
> *B* **Blue.**

> *A* What color are **his shoes**?
> *B* **Brown.**

C Talk with a partner. Choose four classmates. Complete
the chart.

Name	red	yellow	green	black	white	brown	blue
Eliza	sweater	socks			shirt		

1 Before you write

A Talk with a partner. Complete the words.

Shopping list

1. <u>s</u> <u>k</u> i r t
2. ___ ___ e s s
3. ___ ___ o e s
4. ___ ___ o u s e
5. ___ ___ e a t e r
6. T- ___ ___ i r t

B Talk with a partner. Look at the picture. Complete the story.

Sun Mi and her children are shopping today. They need

clothes for school. Sun Mi needs a _____<u>dress</u>_____ and
                                              1

_____ . Her son, Roger, needs a _____
        2   3

and a _____ . Her daughter, Emily, needs a
              4

_____ and a _____ .
        5   6

2 Write

A Write. Complete the shopping list for Sun Mi's family.

Name	Clothing
Sun Mi:	a dress
Emily:	
Roger:	

B Circle the clothes you and your family need.

a blouse	socks	a tie	a dress
a sweater	a jacket	a skirt	a raincoat
a T-shirt	a shirt	shoes	pants

C Write a shopping list for your family.

Name	Clothing

3 After you write

Talk with a partner. Share your writing.

Another view

1 Life-skills reading

The Clothes Place
271 Center Street
Tampa, Florida 33601
(813) 555-7200

Shoes. $29.99	
T-shirt. $7.99	
Subtotal:	$37.98
Tax:	$2.66
Total: $40.64	

Thank you for shopping at
The Clothes Place.
Have a nice day!

A Read the sentences. Look at the receipt. Circle the answers.

1. The Clothes Place is a ____ .
   a. clothing store
   b. supermarket

2. The phone number is ____ .
   a. 555-0072
   b. 555-7200

3. The shoes are ____ .
   a. $19.99
   b. $29.99

4. The tax is ____ .
   a. $2.66
   b. $40.64

B Talk with a partner.

Where do you buy clothes?

2 Fun with language

Write the words in the puzzle. Some words are across (→). Some words are down (↓).

Across →   Down ↓

3 Wrap up

Complete the **Self-assessment** on page 147.

Lesson A Get ready

1 Talk about the picture

A Look at the picture. What do you see?

B Listen and point: cashier • custodian • mechanic
receptionist • salesperson • waiter

2 Listening

SELF-STUDY AUDIO CD **A** 💿 **Listen and repeat.**

1. cashier 2. custodian 3. mechanic
4. receptionist 5. salesperson 6. waiter

SELF-STUDY AUDIO CD **B** 💿 **Listen and circle.**

1 a.  (b.)

2 a.  b.

3 a.  b.

4 a.  b.

Listen again. Check your answers.

C **Talk with a partner.** Point to a picture.
Your partner says the word.

Waiter.

Lesson B *Job duties*

1 Vocabulary focus

Listen and repeat.

1

She answers the phone.

2

CASHIER
She counts money.

3
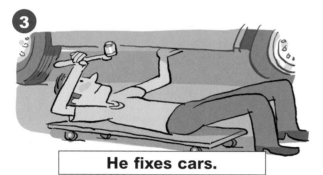
He fixes cars.

4

CUSTODIAN
He cleans buildings.

5

SALE Today
She sells clothes.

6

He serves food.

2 Practice

A Read and match.

1. A receptionist —— sells clothes.
2. A salesperson   cleans buildings.
3. A cashier   answers the phone.
4. A waiter   fixes cars.
5. A custodian   serves food.
6. A mechanic   counts money.

B 💿 **Listen and repeat.** Then write.

answers the phone	cleans buildings	counts money
fixes cars	sells clothes	serves food

Name	Duty
1. Sandra	She _counts money_ .
2. Stephanie	She _____ .
3. Alba	She _____ .

Name	Duty
4. Oscar	He _____ .
5. Tim	He _____ .
6. Ahmad	He _____ .

Talk with a partner. Ask and answer.

A What does **Sandra** do?
B **She counts money.**

3 Communicate

Talk with your classmates. Ask and answer.

A What do you do?
B I'm a **cashier**. I **count money**.

Useful language
What do you do? = What's your job?

1 Grammar focus: *does* and *doesn't*

| Does | he
she | sell clothes? | | Yes, | he
she | does. | | No, | he
she | doesn't. | | doesn't =
does not |

2 Practice

A Read and circle. Then write.

1

A Does he serve food?

B No, he ___*doesn't*___ .
　　　　does (doesn't)

2

A Does he clean buildings?

B Yes, he _____ .
　　　　does　doesn't

3

A Does she answer the phone?

B Yes, she _____ .
　　　　does　doesn't

4

A Does he sell clothes?

B Yes, he _____ .
　　　　does　doesn't

5

A Does she fix cars?

B No, she _____ .
　　　　does　doesn't

🔘 **Listen and repeat.** Then practice with a partner.

B  **Listen and repeat.** Then write.

1. **A** What's his job?
   B _Does_ he _sell_ clothes?
   A _No_ , he _doesn't_ .

2. **B** _____ he _____ cars?
   A _____ , he _____ .

3. **B** _____ he _____ buildings?
   A _____ , he _____ .

4. **B** _____ he _____ food?
   A _____ , he _____ .

5. **B** _____ he _____ money?
   A _____ , he _____ .

6. **B** _____ he _____ the phone?
   A _____ , he _____ .

Talk with a partner. Ask and guess.

> **A** What's his job?
> **B** He's a _____ .

cashier	custodian
mechanic	receptionist
salesperson	waiter

3 Communicate

Talk with your classmates. Play a game. Ask and guess.

> **A** Do you **sell clothes**?
> **B** **No.**
> **A** Do you **fix cars**?
> **B** **Yes.**
> **A** You're a **mechanic**?
> **B** Right.

Lesson D Reading

1 Before you read

Talk about the picture.
What do you see?

2 Read

  Listen and read.
SELF-STUDY AUDIO CD

Shop Smart Employee of the Month:

Sara Lopez

Congratulations, Sara Lopez – Employee of the Month! Sara is a salesperson. She sells clothes. Sara's whole family works here at Shop Smart. Her father is a custodian, and her mother is a receptionist. Her Uncle Eduardo is a waiter. He serves food. Her sister, Lucy, is a cashier. She counts money. Her brother, Leo, fixes cars. He's a mechanic. Everybody in the store knows the Lopez family!

3 After you read

Write the job and the job duty.

1 $hop $mart
Name: Leo Lopez   Job: mechanic
Job duty: He fixes cars.

2 $hop $mart
Name: Lucy Lopez   Job: _____
Job duty: _____

3 $hop $mart
Name: Eduardo Lopez   Job: _____
Job duty: _____

4 $hop $mart
Name: Sara Lopez   Job: _____
Job duty: _____

4 Picture dictionary — Jobs

1 bus driver

2 housewife

3 painter

4 plumber

5 teacher's aide

6 truck driver

SELF-STUDY AUDIO CD **A** 🔊 **Listen and repeat.** Look at the picture dictionary.

B Talk with a partner. Point and ask. Your partner answers.

> *A* What does **he** do?
> *B* He's a **teacher's aide**.

1 Before you write

A **Talk with a partner.** Check (✓) the job duty.

	Counts money	Drives a bus	Cleans buildings	Answers the phone	Serves food
cashier	✓				
custodian					
waiter					
bus driver					
receptionist					

B **Talk with a partner.** Complete the words.

1. s a l e s p _e_ _r_ s o n
2. s e l l s ___ ___ o t h e s
3. m e ___ ___ a n i c
4. f i x ___ ___ c a r s
5. a n ___ ___ e r s t h e p h o n e
6. c ___ ___ n t s m o n e y

C **Read the letter.**

Dear Grandpa,

How are you? We are all well here. Luis and Maria have new jobs! Luis is a waiter. He serves food. Maria is a receptionist. She answers the phone. I'm a housewife. I'm at home.

Write soon.

Love,
Rosa

2 Write

A Talk with a partner. Complete the letter. Use the words from 1B.

Dear Grandma,

How are you? We are all well here. Janie and Walter have new jobs! Janie is a <u>salesperson</u> . She _____ clothes. She also
1   2
_____ the phone at work, and she _____ money.
3   4
Walter is a _____ . He _____ cars.
5   6

Write soon.

Love,
Meg

B Write about your family and friends. Write about their jobs.

1. My friend's name is _____ .

   She is a _____ .

   She _____ .

2. My _____ 's name is _____ .

   He is a _____ .

   He _____ .

3. My _____ 's name is _____ .

   He is a _____ .

   He _____ .

3 After you write

Talk with a partner. Share your writing.

Another view

1 Life-skills reading

HELP WANTED

JOB A	JOB B
Salesperson $10.00 an hour Monday and Wednesday Call 555-1188.	Painter Acme Paint Company Call 555-8491. Part-time work

JOB C	JOB D
Cashier $12.00 an hour Shop Smart E-mail: ShopSmart@cambridge.org	Bus Driver City Bus Company Work mornings. Call evenings: 555-7654

A Read the sentences. Look at the ads. Circle the answers.

1. Job A is for a ____ .
   a. receptionist
   b. salesperson

2. Job B is for a ____ .
   a. painter
   b. plumber

3. For Job C, ____ .
   a. call Shop Smart
   b. write to Shop Smart

4. Call City Bus Company ____ .
   a. in the morning
   b. in the evening

B Talk with a partner.

What job do you want?

2 Fun with language

A Read and match.

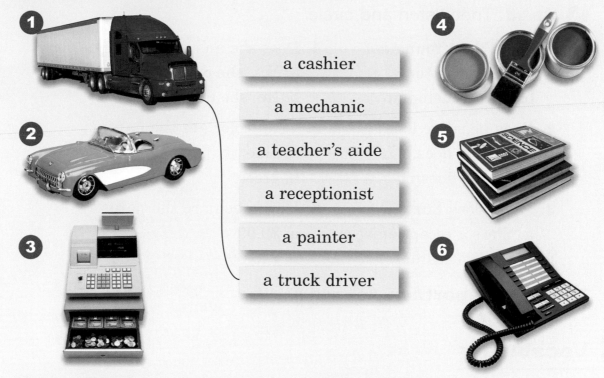

1
2
3

a cashier

a mechanic

a teacher's aide

a receptionist

a painter

a truck driver

4
5
6

Talk with a partner. Compare your answers.

B Circle the words in the puzzle.

answer	cashier	clean	count	custodian
fix	mechanic	sell	waiter	

t	f	i	x	a	b	c	o	u	n	t	q
f	g	m	e	c	h	a	n	i	c	r	o
w	a	i	t	e	r	c	c	l	e	a	n
d	s	e	a	n	s	w	e	r	u	b	a
s	e	l	l	c	a	s	h	i	e	r	
t	r	c	u	s	t	o	d	i	a	n	r

3 Wrap up

Complete the **Self-assessment** on page 148.

1 Listening

Read. Then listen and circle.

1. What does Young do?
   (a.) He's a waiter.
   b. He's a custodian.

2. Does he serve food?
   a. Yes, he does.
   b. No, he doesn't.

3. What does Luz do?
   a. She's a receptionist.
   b. She's a cashier.

4. Does she answer the phone?
   a. Yes, she does.
   b. No, she doesn't.

5. What color are the pants?
   a. blue
   b. green

6. How much are the pants?
   a. $9.99
   b. $19.99

Talk with a partner. Ask and answer.

2 Vocabulary

Write. Complete the story.

| cars | clothes | mechanic | $9.99 | salesperson | shirt |

A New Shirt

Sam is a ___*mechanic*___ . He fixes _____ .
                    1   2

Today he is at Shop Smart. He needs a blue _____ .
                                                    3

Shirts are on sale. Brenda is a _____ . She sells
                                        4

_____ at Shop Smart. How much is the shirt?
      5

It's _____ .
          6

3 Grammar

A Complete the sentences. Use *is* or *are*.

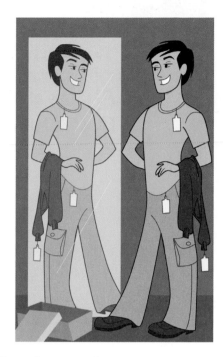

1. **A** How much ___is___ the T-shirt?
   B $10.99.

2. **A** How much _____ the pants?
   B $22.99.

3. **A** How much _____ the shoes?
   B $19.99.

4. **A** How much _____ the sweater?
   B $12.99.

B Read and circle. Then write.

1. **A** Does Kayla count money?
   B Yes, she ___does___ .
   (does) doesn't

2. **A** Does she clean buildings?
   B No, she _____ .
   does   doesn't

3. **A** Does Allen fix cars?
   B No, he _____ .
   does   doesn't

4. **A** Does he serve food?
   B Yes, he _____ .
   does   doesn't

4 Pronunciation

A 💿 Listen to the *e* sound, the *i* sound, and the *u* sound.

e	i	u
red	six	bus

B 💿 Listen and repeat.

e	red	when

i	six	his

u	bus	much

Talk with a partner. Say a word. Your partner points. Take turns.

C 💿 Listen and check (✓).

	e	i	u		e	i	u		e	i	u		e	i	u		e	i	u
1.	✓			2.				3.				4.				5.			

Lesson A Get ready

1 Talk about the picture

A Look at the picture. What do you see?

B 💿 Listen and point: doing homework • doing the laundry
drying the dishes • making lunch
making the bed • washing the dishes

Huan

2 Listening

  A **Listen and repeat.**

1. doing homework 2. doing the laundry 3. drying the dishes
4. making lunch 5. making the bed 6. washing the dishes

  B **Listen and circle.**

1 (a.)  b.

2 a.  b.

3 a.  b.

4 a.  b.

Doing the laundry.

Listen again. Check your answers.

C **Talk with a partner.** Point to a picture.
Your partner says the words.

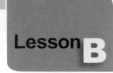

Lesson B Outside chores

1 Vocabulary focus

💿 **Listen and repeat.**

1 cutting the grass

2 getting the mail

3 taking out the trash

4 walking the dog

5 washing the car

6 watering the grass

2 Practice

A Read and match.

taking out the trash   washing the car   cutting the grass

1

2

3

watering the grass   getting the mail   walking the dog

B ☼ Listen and repeat. Then write.

Name	Chore
1. Mrs. Navarro	_____*watering*_____ the grass
2. Mr. Navarro	_____ the grass
3. Roberto	_____ the car
4. Diego	_____ _____ the trash
5. Norma	_____ the mail
6. Rita	_____ the dog

Talk with a partner. Ask and answer.

> **A** What is **Mrs. Navarro** doing?
> **B** **Watering the grass.**

3 Communicate

Talk with a partner. Act and guess.

Watering the grass?

That's right.

Lesson C — *What are they doing?*

1 Grammar focus: questions with *What*

What	is is are	he she they	doing?

Cutting the grass.
Walking the dog.
Washing the dishes.

2 Practice

A Read and circle. Then write.

1. **A** What **_are_** they doing?
   <u>is</u> (are)
   B Making dinner.

   A What _____ he doing?
   is   are
   B Washing the dishes.

2. **A** What _____ they doing?
   is   are
   B Making the bed.

   A What _____ he doing?
   is   are
   B Taking out the trash.

3. **A** What _____ he doing?
   is   are
   B Washing the car.

   A What _____ she doing?
   is   are
   B Watering the grass.

🔊 **Listen and repeat.** Then practice with a partner.

B 🔊 Listen and repeat. Then write.

cutting	doing	drying	getting	making	taking

1 _getting_ the mail

2 _____ lunch

3 _____ the grass

4 _____ the laundry

5 _____ the dishes

6 _____ out the trash

Talk with a partner. Ask and answer.

> **A** What **are they** doing?
> **B** Getting the mail.

> **A** What **is he** doing?
> **B** Making lunch.

3 Communicate

Draw. Ask and guess.

What are they doing?   Drying the dishes.

1 Before you read

Talk about the picture.
What do you see?

2 Read

 SELF-STUDY AUDIO CD **Listen and read.**

Dear Susie,

It's after dinner. My family is working in the kitchen. My daughter Li is washing the dishes. My daughter Mei is drying the dishes. My sons are taking out the trash. Where is my husband? He isn't in the kitchen. He is sleeping in the living room! I am not happy.

I need help. What can I do?

Huan

3 After you read

Read and match.

They are taking out the trash.

She is drying the dishes.

She is washing the dishes.

She is not happy.

4 Picture dictionary — Rooms of a house

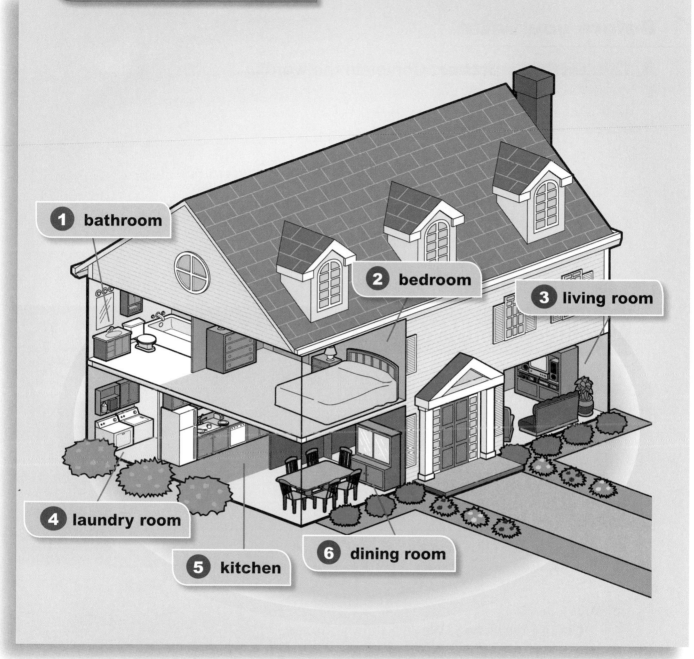

1 bathroom

2 bedroom

3 living room

4 laundry room

5 kitchen

6 dining room

SELF-STUDY AUDIO CD **A** ✹ **Listen and repeat.** Look at the picture dictionary.

B Talk with a partner. Point to a room and ask. Your partner answers.

> *A* What room is this?
> *B* The **kitchen**.

Writing

1 Before you write

A Talk with a partner. Complete the words.

1. d _o_ ing   the   _l_ a u n d r y
2. m ___ king   the   ___ e d s
3. w ___ lking   the   ___ o g
4. c ___ tting   the   ___ r a s s
5. w ___ shing   the   ___ i s h e s
6. t ___ king   out   the   ___ r a s h

B Talk with a partner. Read the chart. Complete the sentences.

Walker Family's Weekend Chores

Chore	Dad	Mom	Max	Iris	Charlie
Do the laundry.		✓		✓	
Take out the trash.					✓
Wash the dishes.			✓		
Cut the grass.	✓				
Make the beds.		✓			
Walk the dog.			✓		✓

It is the weekend. We are doing chores.

1. Charlie is ___ _taking_ ___ _out_ ___ _the_ ___ _trash_ ___ .
2. Mom and Iris are _____ _____ _____ .
3. Dad is _____ _____ _____ .
4. Max is _____ _____ _____ .
5. Mom is _____ _____ _____ .
6. Charlie and Max are _____ _____ _____ .

2 Write

A **Complete the chart.** Write the weekend chores at your house. Check (✓) the names.

My Family's Weekend Chores

Chore	Name			

B **Write.** It is the weekend. Tell about your family's chores. Look at 1B for help.

> **It is the weekend. We are doing chores.**
>
> 1. I am _____ .
>
> 2. _____ is _____ .
>
> 3. _____ is _____ .
>
> 4. _____ is _____ .
>
> 5. _____ and _____ are _____
>
> _____ .

3 After you write

Talk with a partner. Share your writing.

Another view

1 Life-skills reading

Friendly Cleaning Service, Inc.
Madison, WI 53714

We do your chores
with a smile!

Work Order for:

1812 Franklin Street

Date: Monday, December 27

Madison, WI 53714

Name	Chore
Alma	dishes
Kay	beds
Ramiro	grass
Cyrus	laundry
Binh	trash

A Read the sentences. Look at the work order.
Circle the answers.

1. Alma is _____ .
   a. cutting the grass
   b. washing the dishes
2. Kay is _____ .
   a. doing the laundry
   b. making the beds
3. Ramiro is _____ .
   a. cutting the grass
   b. taking out the trash
4. Binh is _____ .
   a. doing the laundry
   b. taking out the trash

B Talk with a partner.

Who does the chores at your house?

2 Fun with language

A Talk with a partner. Complete the chart.

the bed	the car	the dishes	the dog
the grass	homework	the laundry	lunch

cut	wash	do	make	dry
			the bed	

B Circle eight -ing words in the puzzle.

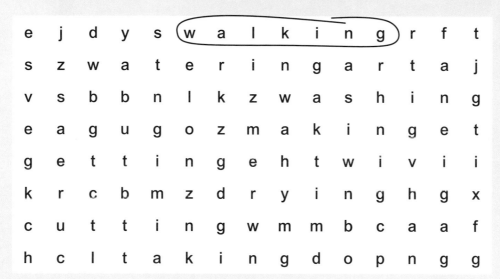

e	j	d	y	s	w	a	l	k	i	n	g	r	f	t
s	z	w	a	t	e	r	i	n	g	a	r	t	a	j
v	s	b	b	n	l	k	z	w	a	s	h	i	n	g
e	a	g	u	g	o	z	m	a	k	i	n	g	e	t
g	e	t	t	i	n	g	e	h	t	w	i	v	i	i
k	r	c	b	m	z	d	r	y	i	n	g	h	g	x
c	u	t	t	i	n	g	w	m	m	b	c	a	a	f
h	c	l	t	a	k	i	n	g	d	o	p	n	g	g

3 Wrap up

Complete the **Self-assessment** on page 149.

Lesson A *Get ready*

1 Talk about the picture

A Look at the picture. What do you see?

B 💿 Listen and point: dance • exercise • fish
play basketball • play cards • swim

Exercise Station

Lupe

2 Listening

A **Listen and repeat.**

1. dance
2. exercise
3. fish
4. play basketball
5. play cards
6. swim

B **Listen and circle.**

1 (a.)  b.

2 a.  b.

3 a.  b.

4 a.  b.

Listen again. Check your answers.

C **Talk with a partner.** Point to a picture. Your partner says the words.

Dance.

1 Vocabulary focus

💿 **Listen and repeat.**

1 cook

2 play the guitar

3 listen to music

4 watch TV

5 read magazines

6 work in the garden

2 Practice

A Read and match.

work in the garden   play the guitar   cook

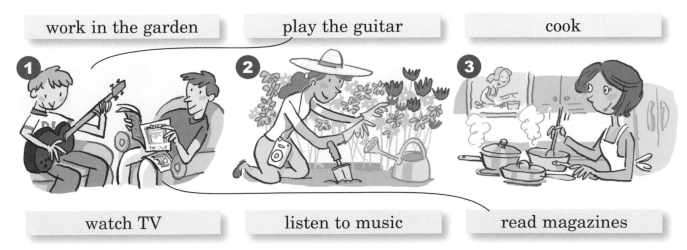

1 watch TV   **2** listen to music   **3** read magazines

B 🔘 **Listen and repeat.** Then write.

cook	listen to music	play the guitar
read magazines	watch TV	work in the garden

Name	Activity
1. Pablo	*watch TV*
2. Tom	
3. Rashid	

Name	Activity
4. Estela	
5. Ling	
6. Farah	

Talk with a partner. Ask and answer.

> *A* What does **Pablo** like to do?
> *B* **Watch TV.**

3 Communicate

Talk with a partner. Act and guess.

> *A* Dance?
> *B* No.
> *A* Play the guitar?
> *B* Right.

I like to watch TV.

1 Grammar focus: *like to*

What	do do does does	you they he she	like to do?

I They He She	like like likes likes	to watch TV.

2 Practice

A Read and circle. Then write.

1

A What do they like to do?

B They ___*like*___ to play basketball.
　　　(like)　likes

2

A What does she like to do?

B She _____ to swim.
　　　like　likes

3

A What does he like to do?

B He _____ to play cards.
　　　like　likes

4

A What does she like to do?

B She _____ to fish.
　　　like　likes

5

A What do they like to do?

B They _____ to dance.
　　　like　likes

🔊 **Listen and repeat.** Then practice with a partner.

B 🔊 **Listen and repeat.**

1. exercise
2. cook
3. play cards
4. work in the garden
5. swim
6. play soccer

Talk with a partner. Ask and answer.

> *A* What **does he** like to do?
> *B* **He likes** to **exercise**.

3 Communicate

Talk with your classmates. Complete the chart.

> *A* What do you like to do, **Vinh**?
> *B* I like to **play basketball**.

Name	What do you like to do?
Vinh	play basketball

Lesson D  Reading

1 Before you read

Talk about the picture.
What do you see?

2 Read

   Listen and read.

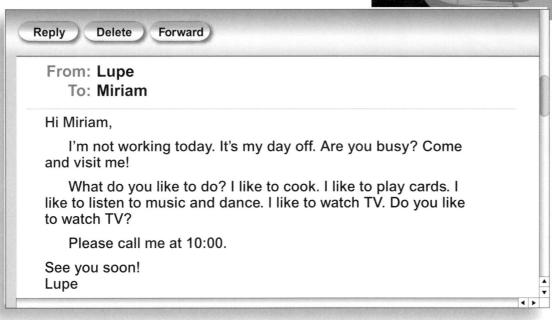

> Reply   Delete   Forward
>
> **From: Lupe**
> **To: Miriam**
>
> Hi Miriam,
>
> I'm not working today. It's my day off. Are you busy? Come and visit me!
>
> What do you like to do? I like to cook. I like to play cards. I like to listen to music and dance. I like to watch TV. Do you like to watch TV?
>
> Please call me at 10:00.
>
> See you soon!
> Lupe

3 After you read

Check (✓) the answers. What does Lupe like to do?

1

2

3

4

5

go to the movies

run

shop

travel

visit friends

volunteer

SELF-STUDY
AUDIO CD

A ◐ **Listen and repeat.** Look at the picture dictionary.

B Talk with a partner. Point and ask. Your partner answers.

> *A* What do they like to do?
> *B* **Go to the movies.**

1 Before you write

A Talk with a partner. Complete the words.

1. r _e_ _a_ d m a g a z i n e s
2. p l ___ ___ b a s k e t b a l l
3. w ___ t c h T V
4. v ___ s ___ t f r i e n d s
5. ___ x e r c i s e
6. w ___ r k ___ n t h e g a r d e n

B Talk with a partner. Write the words.

_____exercise_____

_____ magazines

_____ basketball

_____ in the garden

_____ friends

_____ TV

2 Write

A Complete the sentences. Look at 1B.

My name is Brian. Saturday is my day off.

1. I like to _____*exercise*_____ in the morning.
2. I like to _____ magazines, too.
3. I like to _____ basketball with my son in the afternoon.
4. I also like to _____ in the garden.
5. I like to _____ friends in the evening.
6. I like to _____ TV at night.

B Check (✓). What do you like to do on your day off?

☐ cook   ☐ play cards
☐ dance   ☐ shop
☐ exercise   ☐ swim
☐ fish   ☐ volunteer
☐ go to the movies   ☐ other: _____

Write about yourself.

My Day Off

1. I like to _____.
2. I like to _____.
3. I like to _____.
4. I like to _____.

3 After you write

Talk with a partner. Share your writing.

Another view

1 Life-skills reading

Valley Senior Center Evening Classes

Guitar class

Learn to play the guitar.
September 3 to November 21
Monday and Wednesday: 7:00 p.m. to 9:00 p.m.
Room 101
$100.00

A Read the sentences. Look at the class description.
Circle the answers.

1. This is for ____ .
   a. a guitar class
   b. an exercise class

2. The class is in Room ____ .
   a. 101
   b. 100

3. The class is in the ____ .
   a. morning
   b. evening

4. The class is ____ .
   a. $100.00
   b. $101.00

B Talk with a partner.

Do you play the guitar?

2 Fun with language

A Talk with a partner. Read and match.

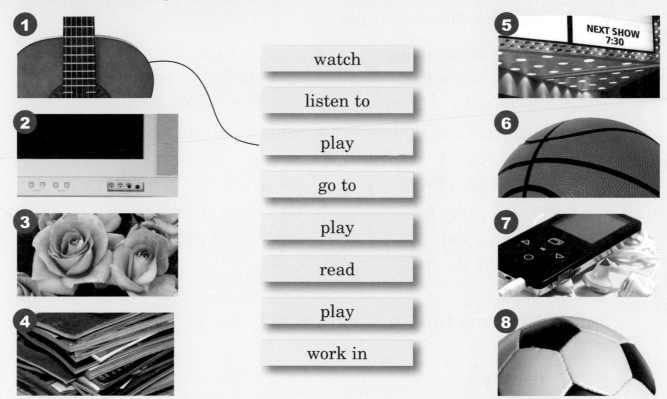

watch

listen to

play

go to

play

read

play

work in

B Talk with a partner. Complete the chart.

	Inside the house	Outside the house
cook	✓	✓
fish		
dance		
shop		
swim		
watch TV		
visit friends		

3 Wrap up

Complete the **Self-assessment** on page 150.

1 Listening

🔘 **Read.** Then listen and circle.

1. What is Marco doing?
   a.) washing the car
   b. playing the guitar

2. What does he like to do?
   a. wash the car
   b. play the guitar

3. What is Ricky doing?
   a. making lunch
   b. making the bed

4. What is Fred doing?
   a. reading magazines
   b. watching TV

5. What does Tina like to do?
   a. cook
   b. exercise

6. What does she like to do on the weekend?
   a. fish
   b. dance

Talk with a partner. Ask and answer.

2 Vocabulary

Write. Complete the story.

| bedroom | kitchen | playing | watching | work |

Sunday at Home

Today is Sunday. My son is ____watching____ TV in the
                              1
living room. My daughter is _____ the guitar in
                                2
her _____ . My wife is in the _____ .
       3   4
She likes to cook. I am in the garden. I like to

_____ in the garden. Sunday is our favorite
       5
day of the week. We like to relax.

3 Grammar

A Complete the sentences. Use *is* or *are*.

1. **A** What ___*are*___ they doing?
   B Drying the dishes.

2. **A** What _____ she doing?
   B Taking out the trash.

3. **A** What _____ he doing?
   B Washing the clothes.

4. **A** What _____ they doing?
   B Getting the mail.

B Read and circle. Then write.

1. **A** What ____*does*____ Pai like to do?
          do (does)
   B He _____ to listen to music.
         like likes

2. **A** What _____ Vance and Anh like to do?
         do does
   B They _____ to read magazines.
         like likes

3. **A** What _____ you like to do?
         do does
   B I _____ to travel.
         like likes

4 Pronunciation

A 💿 Listen to the two sounds of *a, e, i, o,* and *u.*

a		e		i		o		u	
name	at	read	red	five	six	phone	on	June	bus

B 💿 Listen and repeat.

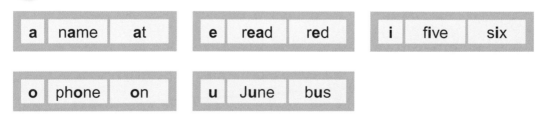

a	name	at

e	read	red

i	five	six

o	phone	on

u	June	bus

Talk with a partner. Say a word. Your partner points. Take turns.

Class list

A Make a chart.

Write the names of three students in your class.

B Talk to the students.

Ask these questions. Write the answers.

1. What's your first name?
2. What's your last name?
3. What's your phone number?

First name	Last name	Phone number
Patricio	Cano	708-555-6737
Lien	Tran	708-555-2986
Phillip	Thomas	708-555-8227

C Share your information.

Make a class booklet.

Shop for school supplies

A Use the Internet.

1. Shop for school supplies near your home.

   Keywords school supplies   (your city)

2. Find a store.
3. Click on the store.

B Make a chart.

Write the name, address, and phone number of the store.

Name	Address	Phone number
Grady's Office Supplies	1865 Mesa Drive	555-2984

C Share your information.

Show your chart to the class. Talk about the stores.

Family chart

A Make a family chart.

On the left, write the names of three students in your class.
Across the top, write the words for family members.

B Talk to the students.

Ask these questions. Check (✓) the answers.

1. Do you have a brother?
2. Do you have a sister?
3. Do you have a husband?
4. Do you have a wife?
5. Do you have a son?
6. Do you have a daughter?

Name	Brother	Sister	Husband	Wife	Son	Daughter
Trong	✓			✓	✓	✓
Hannah	✓	✓	✓			
Nasser				✓		✓

C Share your information.

Show your chart to the class. Talk about the family members.

Find a health clinic

A Use the Internet.

1. Find a health clinic near your home.

Keywords | health clinics | | (your city) |

2. Click on the health clinic.

B Make a chart.

Write the name, address, and phone number of the health clinic.

Name	Address	Phone number
People's Health Clinic	600 Hill Street	555-2381

C Share your information.

Show your chart to the class. Talk about the clinic.

Community map

A Think of a street near your school.

Write the name of the street. Write the names of four places on the street.

B Draw a map of the street.

Draw the places on your map. Write the names on the map.

Main Street Library	City Adult School	Simon's Supermarket

Main Street

United Bank	Main Street Post Office

C Share your information.

Put your map on the wall. Talk about your map.

Library hours

A Use the Internet.

1. Find a library near your home.

Keywords | public libraries | | (your city) |

2. Click on the library.
3. Find the hours for the library.

B Make a chart.

Write the name, address, and hours of the library.

Name	Address	Hours
Millwood Branch Library	64000 Anderson Lane	10:00 a.m. to 7:00 p.m.

C Share your information.

Show your chart to the class. Talk about the library.

A shopping center

A Use the Internet.

1. Find a shopping center near your home.

Keywords | shopping centers | | (your city) |

2. Click on the shopping center.

B Make a chart.

Write the name and address
of the shopping center.

Name	Address
Greenfield Mall	12080 Highway 49

C Share your information.

Show your chart to the class.
Talk about the shopping center.

Find a job

A Make a list.

Write three jobs you want.

1.	receptionist
2.	teacher's aide
3.	mechanic

B Make a chart.

Read the help-wanted ads in the newspaper.

Cut out one ad.

Write the name of the job, the place, and the phone number.

Job	Place	Phone number
receptionist	Caldwell Industries, Inc.	555-8273

C Share your information.

Find a picture of the job.

Read the ad to the class.

Make a class poster with the ad and the picture.

Class survey

A Make a chart.

Write the names of three students in your class. Write four chores.

B Talk to the students.

Ask questions like these. Check (✓) the answers.

1. Do you get the mail?   3. Do you do the laundry?
2. Do you take out the trash?   4. Do you wash the dishes?

Name	Get the mail	Take out the trash	Do the laundry	Wash the dishes
Stacy	✓			✓
Park	✓	✓	✓	
Aiko				✓

C Share your information.

Show your chart to the class. Talk about your classmates' chores.

A movie theater

A Use the Internet.

1. Find a movie theater near your home.

   Keywords | movie theaters | | (your city) |

2. Click on the movie theater.

B Make a chart.

Write the name, address, and phone number of the movie theater. Write the name of a movie.

Name	Address	Phone number	Movie
Plaza Cinema	87 Stone Road	555-7865	Star Wars

C Share your information.

Show your chart to the class. Talk about the theater and movie.

Self-assessments

Unit 1 Personal information

A Vocabulary Check (✓) the words you know.

- ☐ area code
- ☐ country
- ☐ first name
- ☐ ID card
- ☐ last name
- ☐ phone number
- ☐ January
- ☐ February
- ☐ March
- ☐ April
- ☐ May
- ☐ June
- ☐ July
- ☐ August
- ☐ September
- ☐ October
- ☐ November
- ☐ December

B Skills Check (✓) *Yes* or *No*.

	Yes	No
I can use *your*, *his*, *her*, and *my*: *What's **your** name? **My** name is Maria.*		
I can read about personal information.		
I can write about myself.		
I can read an ID card.		

C What's next? Choose one.

- ☐ I am ready for the unit test.
- ☐ I need more practice with _____ .

Unit 2 At school

A Vocabulary Check (✓) the words you know.

☐ book	☐ dictionary	☐ pen
☐ chair	☐ eraser	☐ pencil
☐ computer	☐ notebook	☐ ruler
☐ desk	☐ paper	☐ stapler

B Skills Check (✓) Yes or No.

	Yes	No
I can use *in* and *on*: *Where's my pencil?* **In** *the desk.* **On** *the desk.*	☐	☐
I can read a memo.	☐	☐
I can write about school supplies.	☐	☐
I can read a class schedule.	☐	☐

C What's next? Choose one.

☐ I am ready for the unit test.

☐ I need more practice with _____ .

Unit 3 Friends and family

A Vocabulary Check (✓) the words you know.

☐ aunt	☐ grandfather	☐ sister
☐ brother	☐ grandmother	☐ son
☐ daughter	☐ husband	☐ uncle
☐ father	☐ mother	☐ wife

B Skills Check (✓) *Yes* or *No*.

	Yes	No
I can ask and answer questions with **Do you have . . . ?**: **Do you have** a sister? **Yes, I do. No, I don't.**		
I can read about a family.		
I can write about my family.		
I can read a housing application.		

C What's next? Choose one.

☐ I am ready for the unit test.
☐ I need more practice with _____ .

Unit 4 Health

A Vocabulary Check (✓) the words you know.

☐ arm	☐ foot	☐ leg
☐ cold	☐ hand	☐ sore throat
☐ eye	☐ head	☐ stomach
☐ fever	☐ headache	☐ stomachache

B Skills Check (✓) *Yes* or *No*.

	Yes	No
I can use singular and plural nouns: **one eye**, **two eyes**		
I can read about health problems.		
I can complete a form.		
I can read a medicine label.		

C What's next? Choose one.

☐ I am ready for the unit test.
☐ I need more practice with _____ .

Unit 5 Around town

A Vocabulary Check (✓) the words you know.

- ☐ bank
- ☐ drugstore
- ☐ hospital
- ☐ laundromat
- ☐ library
- ☐ movie theater
- ☐ post office
- ☐ restaurant
- ☐ school
- ☐ senior center
- ☐ street
- ☐ supermarket

B Skills Check (✓) Yes or No.

	Yes	No
I can use **on**, **next to**, **across from**, and **between**: *Where's the school?* **Next to** *the bank.*		
I can read a notice about a new library.		
I can write about the buildings on a street.		
I can read a map.		

C What's next? Choose one.

- ☐ I am ready for the unit test.
- ☐ I need more practice with _____ .

Unit 6 Time

A Vocabulary Check (✓) the words you know.

☐ appointment	☐ class	☐ meeting
☐ at midnight	☐ in the afternoon	☐ movie
☐ at night	☐ in the evening	☐ party
☐ at noon	☐ in the morning	☐ program

B Skills Check (✓) *Yes* or *No*.

	Yes	No
I can ask and answer *yes / no* questions with **be**: *Is your class at 11:00?* **Yes, it is. No, it isn't.**	☐	☐
I can read about a schedule.	☐	☐
I can write about my schedule.	☐	☐
I can read an invitation.	☐	☐

C What's next? Choose one.

☐ I am ready for the unit test.
☐ I need more practice with _____ .

Unit 7 Shopping

A Vocabulary Check (✓) the words you know.

- [ ] blouse
- [ ] dress
- [ ] jacket
- [ ] pants
- [ ] raincoat
- [ ] shirt
- [ ] shoes
- [ ] skirt
- [ ] socks
- [ ] sweater
- [ ] tie
- [ ] T-shirt

B Skills Check (✓) Yes or No.

	Yes	No
I can ask questions with **How much**: **How much is** the shirt? **How much are** the shoes?		
I can read an e-mail.		
I can write a shopping list.		
I can read a receipt.		

C What's next? Choose one.

- [ ] I am ready for the unit test.
- [ ] I need more practice with _____ .

Unit 8 Work

A Vocabulary Check (✓) the words you know.

☐ answer the phone	☐ custodian	☐ salesperson
☐ cashier	☐ fix cars	☐ sell clothes
☐ clean buildings	☐ mechanic	☐ serve food
☐ count money	☐ receptionist	☐ waiter

B Skills Check (✓) *Yes* or *No*.

	Yes	No
I can ask and answer questions with *does*: *Does* he *sell* clothes? **Yes**, he **does**. **No**, he **doesn't**.	☐	☐
I can read an article.	☐	☐
I can write about jobs.	☐	☐
I can read a help-wanted ad.	☐	☐

C What's next? Choose one.

☐ I am ready for the unit test.
☐ I need more practice with _____ .

Unit 9 Daily living

A **Vocabulary** Check (✓) the words you know.

- ☐ cut the grass
- ☐ do homework
- ☐ do the laundry
- ☐ dry the dishes
- ☐ get the mail
- ☐ make lunch
- ☐ make the bed
- ☐ take out the trash
- ☐ walk the dog
- ☐ wash the car
- ☐ wash the dishes
- ☐ water the grass

B **Skills** Check (✓) *Yes* or *No*.

	Yes	No
I can ask and answer questions with *What*: *What is he doing? What are they doing? Talking.*		
I can read a letter about what people are doing.		
I can write about what people are doing.		
I can read a work order.		

C **What's next?** Choose one.

- ☐ I am ready for the unit test.
- ☐ I need more practice with _____ .

Unit 10 Leisure

A Vocabulary Check (✓) the words you know.

- ☐ cook
- ☐ dance
- ☐ exercise
- ☐ fish
- ☐ listen to music
- ☐ play basketball
- ☐ play cards
- ☐ play the guitar
- ☐ read magazines
- ☐ swim
- ☐ watch TV
- ☐ work in the garden

B Skills Check (✓) Yes or No.

	Yes	No
I can ask and answer questions with *like to*: *What do you like to do? I like to swim.*	☐	☐
I can read an e-mail from a friend.	☐	☐
I can write about what I like to do.	☐	☐
I can read a course description.	☐	☐

C What's next? Choose one.

- ☐ I am ready for the unit test.
- ☐ I need more practice with _____ .

Reference

Possessive adjectives

Questions				Answers		
	my				My	
	your				Your	
	his				His	
What's	her	phone number?			Her	phone number is 555-3348.
	its				Its	
	our				Our	
	your				Your	
	their				Their	

Simple present of *have*

Yes / No questions

Do	I	
Do	you	
Does	he	
Does	she	
Does	it	have a laundry room?
Do	we	
Do	you	
Do	they	

Short answers

Yes,			No,		
	I	do.		I	don't.
	you	do.		you	don't.
	he	does.		he	doesn't.
	she	does.		she	doesn't.
	it	does.		it	doesn't.
	we	do.		we	don't.
	you	do.		you	don't.
	they	do.		they	don't.

don't = do not
doesn't = does not

Present of *be*

Am	I	
Are	you	
Is	he	
Is	she	
Is	it	from Somalia?
Are	we	
Are	you	
Are	they	

Short answers

	I	am.		I'm not.
	you	are.		you aren't.
	he	is.		he isn't.
	she	is.		she isn't.
Yes,	it	is.	No,	it isn't.
	we	are.		we aren't.
	you	are.		you aren't.
	they	are.		they aren't.

aren't = are not
isn't = is not

Contractions

I'm = I am
You're = You are
He's = He is
She's = She is
It's = It is
We're = We are
You're = You are
They're = They are

Present continuous

Questions with *What*   **Short answers**

	am	I		
	are	you		
	is	he		
What	is	she	doing?	Working.
	is	it		
	are	we		
	are	you		
	are	they		

Simple present of *like to* + verb

Questions with *What*

What	do	I	like to do?
	do	you	
	does	he	
	does	she	
	does	it	
	do	we	
	do	you	
	do	they	

Answers

	I	like	to swim.
	You	like	
	He	likes	
	She	likes	
	It	likes	
	We	like	
	You	like	
	They	like	

Yes / No questions

Do	I	like to swim?
Do	you	
Does	he	
Does	she	
Does	it	
Do	we	
Do	you	
Do	they	

Short answers

Yes,	I	do.	No,	I	don't.
	you	do.		you	don't.
	he	does.		he	doesn't.
	she	does.		she	doesn't.
	it	does.		it	doesn't.
	we	do.		we	don't.
	you	do.		you	don't.
	they	do.		they	don't.

Cardinal numbers

0 zero	12 twelve	24 twenty-four	36 thirty-six
1 one	13 thirteen	25 twenty-five	37 thirty-seven
2 two	14 fourteen	26 twenty-six	38 thirty-eight
3 three	15 fifteen	27 twenty-seven	39 thirty-nine
4 four	16 sixteen	28 twenty-eight	40 forty
5 five	17 seventeen	29 twenty-nine	50 fifty
6 six	18 eighteen	30 thirty	60 sixty
7 seven	19 nineteen	31 thirty-one	70 seventy
8 eight	20 twenty	32 thirty-two	80 eighty
9 nine	21 twenty-one	33 thirty-three	90 ninety
10 ten	22 twenty-two	34 thirty-four	100 one hundred
11 eleven	23 twenty-three	35 thirty-five	1,000 one thousand

Ordinal numbers

1st first	9th ninth	17th seventeenth	25th twenty-fifth
2nd second	10th tenth	18th eighteenth	26th twenty-sixth
3rd third	11th eleventh	19th nineteenth	27th twenty-seventh
4th fourth	12th twelfth	20th twentieth	28th twenty-eighth
5th fifth	13th thirteenth	21st twenty-first	29th twenty-ninth
6th sixth	14th fourteenth	22nd twenty-second	30th thirtieth
7th seventh	15th fifteenth	23rd twenty-third	31st thirty-first
8th eighth	16th sixteenth	24th twenty-fourth	

Metric equivalents

1 inch = 25 millimeters	1 dry ounce = 28 grams	1 fluid ounce = 30 milliliters
1 foot = 30 centimeters	1 pound = .45 kilograms	1 quart = .95 liters
1 yard = .9 meters	1 mile = 1.6 kilometers	1 gallon = 3.8 liters

Converting Fahrenheit temperatures to Celsius

Subtract 30 and divide by 2:   80°F = approximately 25°C

Countries and nationalities

Afghanistan	Afghan	Georgia	Georgian	Poland	Polish
Albania	Albanian	Germany	German	Portugal	Portuguese
Algeria	Algerian	Ghana	Ghanaian	Puerto Rico	Puerto Rican
Angola	Angolan	Greece	Greek	Republic of	Congolese
Argentina	Argentine	Grenada	Grenadian	the Congo	
Armenia	Armenian	Guatemala	Guatemalan	Romania	Romanian
Australia	Australian	Guyana	Guyanese	Russia	Russian
Austria	Austrian	Haiti	Haitian	Saudi Arabia	Saudi
Azerbaijan	Azerbaijani	Herzegovina	Herzegovinian	Senegal	Senegalese
Bahamas	Bahamian	Honduras	Honduran	Serbia	Serbian
Bahrain	Bahraini	Hungary	Hungarian	Sierra Leone	Sierra Leonean
Bangladesh	Bangladeshi	India	Indian	Singapore	Singaporean
Barbados	Barbadian	Indonesia	Indonesian	Slovakia	Slovak
Belarus	Belarussian	Iran	Iranian	Somalia	Somali
Belgium	Belgian	Iraq	Iraqi	South Africa	South African
Belize	Belizean	Ireland	Irish	South Korea	Korean
Benin	Beninese	Israel	Israeli	Spain	Spanish
Bolivia	Bolivian	Italy	Italian	Sri Lanka	Sri Lankan
Bosnia	Bosnian	Jamaica	Jamaican	Sudan	Sudanese
Brazil	Brazilian	Japan	Japanese	Sweden	Swedish
Bulgaria	Bulgarian	Jordan	Jordanian	Switzerland	Swiss
Cambodia	Cambodian	Kazakhstan	Kazakhstani	Syria	Syrian
Cameroon	Cameroonian	Kenya	Kenyan	Tajikistan	Tajikistani
Canada	Canadian	Kuwait	Kuwaiti	Tanzania	Tanzanian
Cape Verde	Cape Verdean	Laos	Laotian	Thailand	Thai
Chile	Chilean	Lebanon	Lebanese	Togo	Togolese
China	Chinese	Liberia	Liberian	Tonga	Tongan
Colombia	Colombian	Lithuania	Lithuanian	Trinidad	Trinidadian
Comoros	Comoran	Macedonia	Macedonian	Tunisia	Tunisian
Costa Rica	Costa Rican	Malaysia	Malaysian	Turkey	Turkish
Côte d'Ivoire	Ivoirian	Mexico	Mexican	Turkmenistan	Turkmen
Croatia	Croatian	Moldova	Moldovan	Uganda	Ugandan
Cuba	Cuban	Morocco	Moroccan	Ukraine	Ukrainian
Dominica	Dominican	Nepal	Nepali	United Arab	Emirati
Dominican	Dominican	Netherlands	Dutch	Emirates	
Republic		New Zealand	New Zealander	United	British
Ecuador	Ecuadorian	Nicaragua	Nicaraguan	Kingdom	
Egypt	Egyptian	Niger	Nigerien	United States	American
El Salvador	Salvadoran	Nigeria	Nigerian	Uruguay	Uruguayan
Equatorial	Equatorial	Norway	Norwegian	Uzbekistan	Uzbekistani
Guinea	Guinean	Pakistan	Pakistani	Venezuela	Venezuelan
Eritrea	Eritrean	Panama	Panamanian	Vietnam	Vietnamese
Ethiopia	Ethiopian	Paraguay	Paraguayan	Yemen	Yemeni
Fiji	Fijian	Peru	Peruvian	Zambia	Zambian
France	French	Philippines	Filipino	Zimbabwe	Zimbabwean

Map of North America

Self-study audio script

Welcome

Page 3, Exercise 2A – Track 2

1. Look.
2. Listen.
3. Point.
4. Repeat.
5. Talk.
6. Write.
7. Read.
8. Circle.
9. Match.

Page 4, Exercise 3A – Track 3

A, B, C, D, E, F, G, H, I, J, K, L, M, N, O, P, Q, R, S, T, U, V, W, X, Y, Z

Page 4, Exercise 3B – Track 4

1. Anita
2. Daniel
3. Mai
4. Franco
5. Lee
6. Hakim

Page 5, Exercise 4A – Track 5

one, two, three, four, five, six, seven, eight, nine, ten, eleven, twelve, thirteen, fourteen, fifteen, sixteen, seventeen, eighteen, nineteen, twenty

Page 5, Exercise 4B – Track 6

1. six
2. eighteen
3. five
4. three
5. twelve
6. eleven
7. fifteen
8. nine

Unit 1: Personal information

Lesson A: Get ready
Page 7, Exercise 2A – Track 7

1. area code
2. country
3. first name
4. ID card
5. last name
6. phone number

Page 7, Exercise 2B – Track 8

1. *A* What's your area code?
   B 201.
2. *A* What's your phone number?
   B 555-5983.
3. *A* What's your first name?
   B Glen.
4. *A* What's your last name?
   B Reyna.

Lesson D: Reading
Page 12, Exercise 2 – Track 9

Welcome!

Meet our new student. His first name is Ernesto. His last name is Delgado. He is from Mexico. Welcome, Ernesto Delgado!

Page 13, Exercise 4A – Track 10

1. January
2. February
3. March
4. April
5. May
6. June
7. July
8. August
9. September
10. October
11. November
12. December

Unit 2: At school

Lesson A: Get ready
Page 19, Exercise 2A – Track 11

1. a book
2. a chair
3. a computer
4. a desk
5. a notebook
6. a pencil

Page 19, Exercise 2B – Track 12

1. *A* What do you need?
   B A pencil.
   A Here. Take this one.
2. *A* What do you need?
   B A notebook.
   A Here. Take this one.
3. *A* What do you need?
   B A book.
   A Here. Take this one.
4. *A* What do you need?
   B A chair.
   A Here. Take this one.

Lesson D: Reading
Page 24, Exercise 2 – Track 13

Sue,
Have fun at school!
You need a pencil. The pencil is in the desk. You need a notebook. The notebook is on my computer. You need a dictionary. It's on your chair. You need an eraser. It's on the desk!
Love,
Mom

Page 25, Exercise 4A – Track 14

1. Monday
2. Tuesday
3. Wednesday
4. Thursday
5. Friday
6. Saturday
7. Sunday

Unit 3: Friends and family

Lesson A: Get ready
Page 33, Exercise 2A – Track 15

1. daughter
2. father
3. grandfather
4. grandmother
5. mother
6. son

Page 33, Exercise 2B – Track 16

1. *A* Who's that?
   B The grandmother.
2. *A* Who's that?
   B The daughter.
3. *A* Who's that?
   B The father.
4. *A* Who's that?
   B The grandfather.

Lesson D: Reading
Page 38, Exercise 2 – Track 17

My Family

My name is Gloria. This is my family. This is my mother. Her name is Natalia. It is her birthday. This is my father. His name is Enrico. This is my husband, Luis. This is our daughter, Lisa. This is our son, Tony. I love my family!

Page 39, Exercise 4A – Track 18

1. baby
2. girl
3. boy
4. teenager
5. woman
6. man

Unit 4: Health

Lesson A: Get ready
Page 45, Exercise 2A – Track 19

1. doctor
2. doctor's office
3. medicine
4. nurse
5. patient

Page 45, Exercise 2B – Track 20

1. *A* What's the matter?
   B I need a nurse.
2. *A* What's the matter?
   B I need a doctor.
3. *A* What's the matter?
   B I need a nurse.
4. *A* What's the matter?
   B I need some medicine.

Lesson D: Reading
Page 50, Exercise 2 – Track 21

At the Doctor's Office

Tony and Mario are at the doctor's office. They are patients. Tony's leg hurts. His head hurts, too. Mario's arm hurts. His hands hurt, too. Tony and Mario are not happy. It is not a good day.

Page 51, Exercise 4A – Track 22

1. a cold
2. a fever
3. a headache
4. a sore throat
5. a stomachache
6. a toothache

Unit 5: Around town

Lesson A: Get ready
Page 59, Exercise 2A – Track 23

1. bank
2. library
3. restaurant
4. school
5. street
6. supermarket

Page 59, Exercise 2B – Track 24

1. *A* Where's the school?
   B The school? It's on Main Street.
   A Thanks.
2. *A* Where's the restaurant?
   B The restaurant? I don't know.
   A OK. Thank you.
3. *A* Where's the library?
   B The library's on Market Street.
   A Thanks a lot.
4. *A* Where's the supermarket?
   B Sorry, I don't know.
   A Thanks, anyway.

Lesson D: Reading
Page 64, Exercise 2 – Track 25

Notice from Riverside Library
Come and visit Riverside Library. The new library opens today. The library is on Main Street. It is across from Riverside Adult School. It is next to K and P Supermarket. It is between K and P Supermarket and Rosie's Restaurant. The library is open from 9:00 to 5:00, Monday, Wednesday, and Friday.

Page 65, Exercise 4A – Track 26

1. by bicycle
2. by bus
3. by car
4. by taxi
5. by train
6. on foot

Unit 6: Time

Lesson A: Get ready
Page 71, Exercise 2A – Track 27

1. seven o'clock
2. nine o'clock
3. ten o'clock
4. ten-thirty
5. two-thirty
6. six-thirty

Page 71, Exercise 2B – Track 28

1. *A* What time is it?
   B It's nine o'clock.
2. *A* Excuse me. What time is it?
   B It's ten-thirty.
3. *A* What time is it?
   B It's two-thirty.

4. *A* Excuse me. What time is it?
   B It's ten o'clock.

Lesson D: Reading
Page 76, Exercise 2 – Track 29

Teresa's Day

Teresa is busy today. Her meeting with her friend Joan is at 10:00. Her doctor's appointment is at 1:00. Her favorite TV program is at 4:30. Her class is at 6:30. Her uncle's birthday party is at 6:30, too. Oh, no! What will she do?

Page 77, Exercise 4A – Track 30

1. in the morning
2. in the afternoon
3. in the evening
4. at night
5. at midnight
6. at noon

Unit 7: Shopping

Lesson A: Get ready
Page 85, Exercise 2A – Track 31

1. a dress
2. pants
3. a shirt
4. shoes
5. socks
6. a T-shirt

Page 85, Exercise 2B – Track 32

1. *A* How much is the shirt?
   B The shirt? Nineteen dollars.
2. *A* How much are the socks?
   B The socks? One ninety-nine.
3. *A* How much is the dress?
   B The dress? Thirty-nine ninety-nine.
4. *A* How much are the pants?
   B The pants? Twenty-four ninety-nine.

Lesson D: Reading
Page 90, Exercise 2 – Track 33

Hi Patty,
This morning, Samuel and I are going to The Clothes Place. Samuel needs blue pants. He needs a tie, too. I need a red dress and black shoes. Dresses are on sale. They're $39.99. Shoes are on sale, too. They're $19.99. That's good.
Call you later,
Rose

Page 91, Exercise 4A – Track 34

1. black
2. white
3. yellow
4. orange
5. brown
6. green
7. blue
8. purple
9. pink
10. red

Unit 8: Work

Lesson A: Get ready
Page 97, Exercise 2A – Track 35

1. cashier
2. custodian
3. mechanic
4. receptionist
5. salesperson
6. waiter

Page 97, Exercise 2B – Track 36

1. *A* What does he do?
   B He's a waiter.
2. *A* What does she do?
   B She's a receptionist.
3. *A* What's his job?
   B He's a custodian.
4. *A* What's her job?
   B She's a mechanic.

Lesson D: Reading
Page 102, Exercise 2 – Track 37

Shop Smart Employee of the Month: Sara Lopez
Congratulations, Sara Lopez – Employee of the Month! Sara is a salesperson. She sells clothes. Sara's whole family works here at Shop Smart. Her father is a custodian, and her mother is a receptionist. Her Uncle Eduardo is a waiter. He serves food. Her sister, Lucy, is a cashier. She counts money. Her brother, Leo, fixes cars. He's a mechanic. Everybody in the store knows the Lopez family!

Page 103, Exercise 4A – Track 38

1. bus driver
2. housewife
3. painter
4. plumber
5. teacher's aide
6. truck driver

Unit 9: Daily living

Lesson A: Get ready
Page 111, Exercise 2A – Track 39

1. doing homework
2. doing the laundry
3. drying the dishes
4. making lunch
5. making the bed
6. washing the dishes

Page 111, Exercise 2B – Track 40

1. *A* What's she doing?
   B She's doing homework.
2. *A* What's he doing?
   B He's washing the dishes.
3. *A* What's she doing?
   B She's making the bed.
4. *A* What's he doing?
   B He's making lunch.

Lesson D: Reading

Page 116, Exercise 2 – Track 41

Dear Susie,

It's after dinner. My family is working in the kitchen. My daughter Li is washing the dishes. My daughter Mei is drying the dishes. My sons are taking out the trash. Where is my husband? He isn't in the kitchen. He is sleeping in the living room! I am not happy.

I need help. What can I do?

Huan

Page 117, Exercise 4A – Track 42

1. bathroom
2. bedroom
3. living room
4. laundry room
5. kitchen
6. dining room

Unit 10: Leisure

Lesson A: Get ready

Page 123, Exercise 2A – Track 43

1. dance
2. exercise
3. fish
4. play basketball
5. play cards
6. swim

Page 123, Exercise 2B – Track 44

1. *A* Do you like to dance?
   B Yes, we do.
2. *A* Do you like to play cards?
   B Yes, we do.
3. *A* What do you like to do?
   B I like to fish.
4. *A* What do you like to do?
   B I like to swim.

Lesson D: Reading

Page 128, Exercise 2 – Track 45

Hi Miriam,

I'm not working today. It's my day off. Are you busy? Come and visit me!

What do you like to do? I like to cook. I like to play cards. I like to listen to music and dance. I like to watch TV. Do you like to watch TV?

Please call me at 10:00. See you soon!

Lupe

Page 129, Exercise 4A – Track 46

1. go to the movies
2. run
3. shop
4. travel
5. visit friends
6. volunteer

Illustration credits

Ken Batelman: 20, 22 (*bottom*), 59 (*top*), 68

Travis Foster: 3, 7 (*bottom*), 19 (*bottom*), 33 (*bottom*), 45 (*bottom*), 49, 55, 61, 85 (*bottom*), 97 (*bottom*), 98, 111 (*top*), 113 (*bottom*), 123 (*bottom*), 124 (*bottom*), 125 (*bottom*)

Chuck Gonzales: 23, 37, 40, 46 (*bottom*), 47 (*top*), 57, 100, 101, 112 (*top*), 113 (*top*), 126, 130

Colin Hayes: 39, 51, 65, 103, 117, 129

Pamela Hobbs: 9, 48, 92, 112 (*bottom*)

Rod Hunt: 60 (*bottom*), 99, 124 (*top*), 125 (*top*)

Ben Kirchner: 2, 6, 12, 18, 24, 32, 33 (*top*), 38, 44, 50, 58, 64 (*top*), 70, 76, 84, 90 (*top*), 96, 102, 110, 116, 122, 128

Victor Kulihin: 13, 25, 77, 91

Frank Montagna: 10, 52, 109, 115

Jason O'Malley: 22 (*top*), 26, 72, 86 (*top*), 87, 90 (*bottom*)

Greg Paprocki: 21, 34, 35, 47 (*bottom*), 89 (*top*), 114

Monika Roe: 7 (*top*), 19 (*top*), 31, 36, 45 (*top*), 59 (*bottom*), 71 (*bottom*), 85 (*top*), 86 (*bottom*), 88, 89 (*bottom*), 97 (*top*), 111 (*bottom*), 123 (*top*)

Phil Williams: 60 (*top*), 62 (*bottom*), 63

Photography credits

3 ©Jupiter Images

4 ©Ian Shaw/Alamy

5 ©Inmagine

11 (*both*) ©Inmagine

14 ©Inmagine

16 ©Inmagine

20 (*clockwise from top left*) ©Jupiter Images; ©Shutterstock; ©Shutterstock; ©Greg Wright/ Alamy; ©Shutterstock; ©D. Hurst/Alamy

24 (*all*) ©George Kerrigan

48 (*all*) ©Inmagine

63 (*top to bottom*) ©Jupiter Images; ©Inmagine

69 (*all*) ©Inmagine

71 ©Inmagine

87 (*clockwise from top left*) ©Inmagine; ©Stephen Oliver/Getty Images; ©Paul Thompson Images/ Alamy; ©Shutterstock; ©Inmagine; ©D. Hurst/ Alamy

95 (*top row, left to right*) ©Inmagine; ©Inmagine; ©Tom Schierlitz/Getty Images; ©Inmagine; (*middle row, left to right*) ©Paul Thompson Images/ Alamy; ©Shutterstock; ©Shutterstock; ©Alamy; (*bottom row, left to right*) ©Susanna Price/Getty Images; ©Dorling Kindersley/Getty Images; ©Inmagine

101 ©Jupiter Images

107 (*clockwise from top left*) ©Inmagine; ©Shutterstock; ©Inmagine; ©Inmagine; ©Jupiter Images; ©Inmagine

127 (*clockwise from top left*) ©Inmagine; ©Jupiter Images; ©Jupiter Images; ©Shutterstock; ©Inmagine; ©Inmagine

128 (*left to right*) ©Jupiter Images; ©George Kerrigan; ©Jupiter Images; ©Inmagine; ©Shutterstock

133 (*clockwise from top left*) ©Shutterstock; ©Inmagine; ©Shutterstock; ©Shutterstock; ©Inmagine; ©Inmagine; ©George Kerrigan; ©Jupiter Images